For my father Bernard who sadly will never get to read this book and to my wife Kirsty for sticking with me throughout the project.

YOUNG PEOPLE + WORSHIP

A PRACTICAL GUIDE

EDITED BY MARK MONTGOMERY

CHURCH HOUSE PUBLISHING

Church House Publishing
Church House
Great Smith Street
London SW1P 3NZ

Tel: 020 7898 1451
Fax: 020 7898 1449

ISBN 978–0–7151–4057–4

Published 2007 by Church House Publishing

Typeset by RefineCatch Limited, Bungay, Suffolk

Printed in England by The Cromwell Press Ltd, Trowbridge, Wiltshire

YOUNG PEOPLE + WORSHIP

SERIES INTRODUCTION

This title is one of a series commissioned by Church House Publishing to explore further the themes of the Church of England's National Youth Strategy, *Good News for Young People* (downloadable from www.cofe.anglican.org/info/education/youth/). The strategy has four main themes: young people and mission, young people and worship, young people as leaders and resourcing youth workers.

These titles are aimed at youth workers and leaders, whether paid or voluntary, and at youth workers in training on the increasing number of professional and degree courses in youth work and ministry. Church leaders and members with an interest in developing their church's work with young people will also find them helpful.

Contributors to each title are experienced practitioners in their field. Each volume offers a mixture of practical tips, reflection, real-life case studies and advice on taking things further. The experiences shared and wisdom offered here are intended to be starting points to stimulate your own thinking and practice, as applied to the situation in which you work.

It is our hope that you will find much here to inspire, and challenge, your work with young people.

YOUNG PEOPLE + WORSHIP: CONTRIBUTORS

Craig Abbott is a Youth Officer in the Diocese of Blackburn. He studied for a degree in Christian ministry before working as a full-time youth worker for nine years in parishes and for a Christian schools-work organization. One of his passions is to enable young people to access authentic expressions of Christianity in their schools and churches.

David Brown is married to Wendy and has two beautiful children, Tom and Poppy. His work as the Youth Officer for the Church of Ireland means key themes are present in his life: travel, beautiful scenery and a deep sense of God at work among many young people and their churches! In the midst of this, he retains a deep interest in politics, reconciliation and the emerging church in Ireland. (To check out more about the Church of Ireland Youth Department, visit their web site www.ciyd.org).

Diane Craven was an English teacher and a freelance writer and educational consultant. She is now Children's Adviser in the Diocese of Southwark and is passionate about theological reflection in work with children and young people. She is a Reader and is working towards a PhD in Theology.

Jean Kerr is currently Bishop's Officer for Mission and Unity and Canon Missioner at Rochester Cathedral. She has spent far too many years to mention in local and diocesan youth work but still regularly mentors young people and has a passion for them to be released into creative styles of ministry.

Richard Lamey wrote this chapter while Assistant Curate in the Stockport South West Team. He is now Priest-in-Charge of St Mary's, Newton, Hyde and a member of the Chester Diocesan Youth Committee. His hobbies do not include bog snorkelling.

Pete Maidment is a Youth and Children's Officer in the Diocese of Winchester. He has been involved in full-time youth ministry for over nine years and has worked in various settings both detached and rural, inside the

Church and out. Pete loves helping young people develop a relationship with Jesus Christ.

Susie Mapledoram is a schools-based Diocesan Youth Officer in Blackburn Diocese. She has a degree in youth and community studies from the University of Birmingham and has worked in a variety of youth-work settings over some years including parish-based youth work, schools work and training youth workers.

Mark Montgomery (Editor) is Youth Officer for the Diocese of Chester. A professionally qualified youth worker, Mark has been working with young people for over ten years, mainly in a mixture of parish and diocesan roles within the Anglican Church. He is also a volunteer youth worker in his local church and passionate about engaging with young people through new forms of worship. He has also worked part-time in secular youth work. Before going into full-time youth work, Mark worked as a designer and ran a freelance design and promotions company.

Tim Sledge is Diocesan Mission Enabler in the Peterborough Diocese, a member of the Archbishops' College of Evangelists and an associate missioner with Fresh Expressions. He was vicar of three parishes in the Wakefield Diocese before moving further south. Tim is co-author of *Youth Emmaus* 1 and 2.

Helen Williams-Carter was the Youth Adviser for the Diocese of Liverpool. She has been involved in full-time youth work for six years and is trained as a primary school teacher. Music has been a major influence on Helen's Christian life and she is passionate to see young people released to express themselves in worship.

FOREWORD

This book will be excellent for church leaders who are beginning to think seriously about how their young people worship. Many youth ministers will be familiar with most of the book's themes, but many people who lead church youth groups might never have thought about the alternative structures and ideas that are considered and suggested here.

There is an excellent first chapter on worship as the whole of life and practical details of going about worship as the body of Christ together. All the way through there is encouragement to plan worship in such a way that young people are active participants rather than passive observers.

The book does not pull any punches in making it clear where practice needs to change, such as the need to address the alienation many young people feel in 'Family Services'. The book also opens up the debate around separate youth congregations. No easy answers are given – but it is good to ask the questions honestly.

Youth ministers are encouraged to think creatively about the connection between Sunday worship experiences and Monday at school. The authors take youth culture seriously but at the same time recognize that young people do not want to dumb down God and be patronized with gimmicks.

This book also exhorts us not to get stuck in our own traditions but to reinterpret them afresh, and includes case studies from real-life situations to inspire us to do just that.

It encourages new attitudes to young people and to worshipping God, with fresh motivation to see it work. It is my hope and prayer that its suggestions will be taken on board.

Bishop Roger Sainsbury
Chair of The National Youth Agency and the Centre for Youth Ministry

(With thanks to Olly Mears and Paul Oxley from my pastoral group at Trinity College, Bristol)

INTRODUCTION

Why another book on youth worship?

The project is one response to the Church of England's National Youth Strategy agreed by Synod in 2002. The aim of this book is to help churches to think about the ways in which they can engage young people in worship, or rethink the ways in which they already do so. My hope is that you will use this book as a resource and thought provoker as you grapple with the issues of engaging young people in worship.

As you read this book you will discover that there is no 'one size fits all' way of engaging young people in worship. I hope that the clichés of youth worship you may have in your mind – the raves, loud music, flashing lights, etc. – will be challenged and you will discover that young people, just like adults, meet with God in a variety of different ways.

All the ideas presented in this book have worked or are working in engaging young people in worship. This is not to say that just because they are working in these particular settings they will work for you, but they provide a starting point for thinking through what might work in your own situation, with the young people in your church or youth group.

This book has been designed to have many access points for youth workers and churches. You will find chapters on all aspects of worship that young people engage in, from traditional and family services to the large youth events that usually take place each summer. Some of the issues raised are not just relevant to young people but should help you think through ways of making worship accessible to the wider community as well.

All the authors are experienced practitioners who are passionate about involving young people in the worshipping life of the Church. Our hope is that you will be inspired to do the same!

How to use this book

Use this book to gain ideas: the projects or activities highlighted are taken from a broad variety of church traditions and settings. They are not all mega-projects, attracting hundreds of young people. Some are comparatively small, taking place in struggling local churches which may be similar to yours!

Use this book as a discussion starter: read the chapters, discuss them, agree with them, disagree with them, be challenged, be dismissive. What is offered here is not necessarily the final word on the subject: we hope your own creative ideas will be sparked off by the content.

The shape of the book

The book has been organized into four Sections:

1. An introduction to worship
2. Creative approaches to liturgy
3. New forms of worship
4. Spirituality.

The book starts with a look at what worship is, and the place of some key aspects of it.

In the next section we look at how the existing liturgy of the Church may be approached more creatively in our work with young people, within traditional services, all-age worship and in services specially created for young people.

In Section 3 we take things further by looking at new and alternative ways of worshipping with young people: from small-scale experimentation in the local church through to youth congregations and examples of alternative worship.

In Section 4 we look at the current hot topic of the spirituality of young people and consider some ways of encouraging young people to develop a Christian spirituality.

To sum up, we consider how we can help young people to develop into life-long worshippers, beyond a Sunday service or a mid-week youth group, beyond the church walls and beyond their teenage years.

The shape of each chapter*

Each chapter is split into a number of sections. **The introduction**, not surprisingly, does exactly what it implies, introduces the theme of the chapter. **The issue** section explores the issue and why the theme of the chapter matters to our understanding of young people and worship. The **theory and background** section then gives an understanding of what is really involved in engaging young people in worship and the theological basis for our understanding. A **need to know** section gives practical understanding and **case studies** seek to put the theme into a context that shows how the theme works in practice. Finally a **thinking it through** section has questions for reflection, mostly aimed at youth or church leaders themselves, but sometimes these questions are also relevant to the young people we work with. This might be a section a youth or church leadership team could use to think through one of the issues raised in the book and how it could impact on their ongoing work. Each chapter ends with a short **summary** and a **taking it further** list of resources, books, web sites and organizations that work in the area addressed, so the issues raised here can be explored more fully. These organizations cover a broad spectrum of work and churchmanship. They are intended as a starting point and do not provide a comprehensive list of those groups engaged in each area. If your favourite group for resourcing a particular issue is not listed, we can only apologize!

A note on terminology

Throughout the book the terms 'youth leader' and 'youth worker' are used interchangeably and do not imply that the leader or worker is paid for their role. Where an issue is particularly relevant for a paid worker that point is clearly made in the text.

Mark Montgomery
September 2006

* Chapters 10 and 11 are linked. Chapter 11 is a more practical response and follow-up to the more theoretical Chapter 10, so these two chapters don't follow the same chapter structure.

AN INTRODUCTION TO WORSHIP

SECTION 1

In this first section, we focus on different aspects of worship. Richard Lamey explores what worship is and what it is not, by questioning four popular myths about young people and worship. Then Helen Williams-Carter considers the place of music in the lives of young people and in worship: how do they relate to each other? And finally in this section Diane Craven examines the role of prayer and word in worship for young people.

1 WHAT IS WORSHIP?

Richard Lamey

INTRODUCTION

What is worship? Life! (Or to put it better, our lives are worship)

Jon, aged 19

THE ISSUE: We worship in church, and we worship by living

Christians are marked with the sign of the cross from their baptism. Because we live in relationship with God, everything that we do is worship. At work or college or school, at play, on holiday, with others and alone, at home and in public, we are worshipping because we are people who belong to God and we cannot separate what we do as Christians and what we do as human beings. We are one: our Christianity is not a coat we can remove as and when we want to. And because we belong to God, because we are redeemed by Christ and filled with his Spirit, our whole lives are worship. That is as true for young people as it is for bishops.

THEORY AND BACKGROUND: What do we mean by worship?

Worship is too easily limited to what happens on Sunday morning in church, too easily limited to what happens when people meet together for a service in the name of Christ at an advertised time in a church building. That *is* worship, but worship is also a wider calling than that. Worship, literally, is giving God his worth. (The word comes from the Old English *weorth*, worth, and *scipe*, ship.)

Properly, fully, worship is the whole of our wholehearted response to the wonderful, majestic, humbling, encouraging reality of God. Worship is our attempt to give God what God deserves. Worship is our attempt to cause God delight by living in his name, to his glory. Worship is what happens when we are conscious of God and long to be closer to him. Worship is standing before God and learning how to live. Worship is that 'yes' which is our heartfelt and instinctive response to the God who made us and loves us and died for us, who lives for us and in us.

When it comes to gathered worship, contrary to the popular myth, it is often young people who are most accepting of the fact that others might worship

> **'Worship is standing before God and learning how to live. Worship is that "yes" which is our heartfelt and instinctive response to the God who made us and loves us and died for us, who lives for us and in us.'**

differently. They are used to having to fit in with what is already there. They are used to churches which think that they're doing something amazing by including a song written in the lifespan of their parents. That many young people faithfully attend churches which make little allowance for them is a testament to their faith and to God's grace.

NEED TO KNOW: Busting the four worship myths!

In this section we will look at what worship is by addressing four popular myths:

Myth 1: Worship is only what happens in church on Sunday.
Myth 2: Worship must meet my need.
Myth 3: Worship is a nice thing to do.
Myth 4: Youth worship is better than other types of worship.

Myth 1: Worship is only what happens in church on Sunday

This adoration should be part of our daily lives and I don't think we particularly need a time of prayer or a sermon to make worship complete. We are worshipping when God has been glorified in us. To worship is to bow down, place yourself in God's hands and submit yourself utterly to him. That can be in prayer or in singing his praise but can also be reflected in our actions – when we serve and put others' needs before our will, that is bowing down, that is worship. Carol, 19

The things of church are worship – but so are acts of service and personal devotion and obedient living and people meeting at work or school to pray together. Life lived in honour of God is worship. Indeed, everything that glorifies God is worship. An Anglican Post-Communion Prayer places our worship in church in the wider context of our service in the world:

Almighty God,
we thank you for feeding us
with the body and blood of your Son Jesus Christ.
Through him we offer you our souls and bodies
to be a living sacrifice.
Send us out in the power of your Spirit
to live and work
to your praise and glory.
Amen.

Common Worship

Gathered worship and worshipful living go together. They are a major concern of the Old Testament prophets. Amos receives a message from God:

> I hate, I despise your festivals, and I take no delight in your solemn assemblies . . . Take away from me the noise of your songs; I will not listen to the melody of your harps. But let justice roll down like waters, and righteousness like an ever-flowing stream. (Amos 5.21, 23, 24)

God will not accept the sacrifice, the praise, of his people unless they stop abusing the poor and the orphan and start to live out what they so lightly say. Micah puts it bluntly and beautifully: 'and what does the Lord require of you but to do justice, and to love kindness, and to walk humbly with your God?' (Micah 6.8). God does not require sacrifice. He requires worshipful living every day. He requires that we learn to see the world as God sees it and to commit ourselves to building our world into the place God longs for it to be. Our concern today is the same, that we must live out what we confess. If we don't, then we are indeed hypocrites.

'God does not require sacrifice. He requires worshipful living every day. He requires that we learn to see the world as God sees it and to commit ourselves to building our world into the place God longs for it to be.'

In worship we communicate with God, experience the work of God's grace in us. In worship we are changed into the image of God. In worship we are converted into residents of the kingdom of heaven. In worship we learn to see the world through the eyes of its Creator. In worship we determine to meet the needs of the world because of who God is and what our love for him has taught us.

The quotations by young people in this chapter are from people who went to Basecamp in 2004, a camp for 16- to 20-year-olds which combines manual work for the National Trust on footpaths and walls with sessions on Christian leadership and living, and acts of worship. In itself Basecamp models this cycle, because the songs which were sung in gathered worship the evening before often resurfaced while walking to the worksite and while it rained on a soggy hillside. What was sung in church strengthened us while we lived, and what we lived out inspired our worship as we thanked God for his great gifts to us.

Worship is the way we live out the two great commandments: 'Love the Lord your God with all your heart and with all your soul, and with all your mind . . . love your neighbour as yourself' (Matthew 22.37–39). Worship is about our actions and our lives, about how we love, about what we do with our money and our time and our political voice. We must live faith as well as say it. In the process we learn more about God.

'Worship is about our actions and our lives, about how we love, about what we do with our money and our time and our political voice. We must live faith as well as say it. In the process we learn more about God.'

There is a definite cycle to this, which can start anywhere. In worship in church and prayer God once more chooses to reveal himself to us. We meet with God and then we go out into the world excited and inspired to live as his followers, to serve others, to make the world a just and a holy place. And in the attempt we learn more of who God is, which calls us back to the praise of God, which as the Authorized Version of the Bible states, is our reasonable service.

Our worship is made up of both public worship and private devotion, prayer and Bible reading and quiet time. Unless we spend time with God, alone and with others, then we will struggle to know where God is at work in the world and how we should join in.

Jesus shows by his own example how gathered worship and worshipful living feed into each other. Again and again in the Gospels Jesus goes to the synagogue to worship and pray. Again and again in the Gospels Jesus makes time to be with his Father. He is in the wilderness for 40 days. He crosses Lake Galilee to avoid the crowds and find time to be with his Father. On the night of his betrayal he goes into the garden of Gethsemane and prays so intently that sweat beads on his brow like blood. He asks Peter and James and John to keep watch with him, to support him as he prays. Time and time again he prays to his Father, and then, when he comes down from the mountain or back from the quiet place, he bursts into action, preaching and healing and announcing that the kingdom of God has come near. Throughout his ministry, we read, Jesus made time to be alone with the Father. How could we do otherwise?

Myth 2: Worship must meet my need

The best worship that I have been to is possibly one Sunday in church, with a real sense of God and peace among everyone. Louise, 17

Over Christmas, immediately after a service, I was cornered by a long-standing member of the congregation who clearly had something to say: 'It's no wonder the Church is dying when you use readings like that.' My crime had been to use a translation of the Bible which had God saying 'Let us make humankind in our image' (Genesis 1.26) rather than 'Let us make man in our image'.

What makes worship difficult is having to worship together. But as Louise said, worshipping with others can also be an immense joy and a way of meeting God. Worship is about what focuses everyone's heart on God, not what I personally find helpful.

Too often we have precise ideas of what works for us, and too little time for what works for others. And yet we are called to worship together. Worship is not a hobby which we share with people who are exactly like us. The Church of God is not made up simply of people who have the same interests as me: the Church of God is the whole people of God. St Paul puts it very graphically when he says that we are not all meant to be eyes or fingers or ears, that we are all meant to be the people God made us to be and to play our unique and vital part in the life of the Church. We are one body together and we have to accept that this need to be together completely outweighs our personal need for gratification. We must worship with others. Meeting together as the family of God is part of what glorifies God.

Worship is not about us or what we like or want or need. It is about God and about what God desires from us. And part of what God desires is a healthy and welcoming community meeting in his name and inspired by his Spirit, which then goes out to transform and leaven the world. My personal preference pales into insignificance compared to that vision.

'Worship is not about us or what we like or want or need. It is about God and about what God desires from us. And part of what God desires is a healthy and welcoming community meeting in his name and inspired by his Spirit, which then goes out to transform and leaven the world.'

Myth 3: Worship is a nice thing to do

Worship works when I come away not thinking about whether I have been emotionally 'uplifted', in fact not focused on what I think at all, but sensing that I have engaged with God, learnt something about him, and feeling an obedience, a humility, a determination to do his will. Carol, 19

Gathered worship is not simply a pleasant way to pass an hour, although it might be. We worship God not for our own sake, not because we think that God is secretly very grateful to us for sparing him the time, but to give glory to God.

We do it, to be honest, because the need flows out of us. Worshipping God is the thing we were made to do, a way in which we discover who we truly are in the sight of God. Worship is life itself. We meet God and he changes us, shows us what is possible, what we can achieve for him. Worship often starts with 'The Lord is here' or 'The Lord be with you.' In that moment we acknowledge the fact that we are in God's presence. We are face to face with God, with the God who made the universe and, amazingly, this God wants to speak to us, wants to be part of our lives. 'Whereas the prophets of old spoke at people, and delivered their uncompromising take-it-or-leave-it messages, Jesus speaks with people, and asks them questions. He is searching for a response, for dialogue.'[1] It is hardly surprising that worship, which is coming face to face with the living God, changes us. If it did not it would mean that we had not engaged with God, not listened to God, not been wholly there in all of our hopes and fears, our strengths and weaknesses.

'It is hardly surprising that worship, which is coming face to face with the living God, changes us. If it did not it would mean that we had not engaged with God, not listened to God, not been wholly there in all of our hopes and fears, our strengths and weaknesses.'

What we do together in worshipping God changes how we see the world and how we live as people of God. Without our gathering in worship there would be no dance, no inspiration, no vision, no stillness, no encounter. Without making time to worship God there is no revelation of what God is calling us to do. Outside the City of Manchester Stadium is an immense sculpture called B of the Bang by the brilliant Thomas Heatherwick. It is the tallest sculpture in the United Kingdom (taller than the Leaning Tower of Pisa) and leans at an angle of 30°, a starburst of angular cocktail sticks. It evokes the moment when the starting pistol fires. It evokes the explosion of the starting pistol and the coiled potential of the athletes. Gathered worship is, for us, the B of the Bang – it inspires us to go into the world and run the race set before us to the glory of God, full of urgency and power and courage. Because we meet with God in worship we know how to dance. And we are sent from the moment of worship and encounter and understanding into the world like glorious fireworks.

Worship teaches us who we are and how we should live. Worshipping God in church is not just a nice thing to do. It is how we know how to live. God engages with us in Scripture and prayer and bread and wine. And we respond in prayer and song and openness: and we are changed. God alters what we think we want into what God wants us to long for and to work for.

We do not leave church the same as we entered church. We meet with God and we are challenged to grow into his likeness, to be (with others) his worshipping, faithful, committed followers. Worship in church is about meeting with God together, and praising God and being transformed. In worship we are forgiven by the God of mercy and restored to life. Worship is also about gazing into the face of God, a hint of the glory of heaven.

Worship is often, hopefully, a nice thing to do – it is also the most important thing we can ever do, not because of what it does for us but because it is our only honest response to God. Worshipping is for God's sake, not our own. Every other effect of worship is but a side-effect.

Myth 4: Youth worship is better than other types of worship

It is often the music that frustrates me, though, in so-called 'worship-sessions'. Often I feel like I am being manipulated, that the musicians are trying to stir up my emotions and make me respond and yet there is no mention of 'truth'. Carol, 19

There is nothing inherently special about what is called youth worship, which is usually a service put together by young people, or for young people. 'Youth worship' can be every bit as formulaic or exhilarating as any other act of worship because young people are every bit as varied and individual as anyone else. Anyone tempted to assume that youth worship is always fresh and exciting because it involves guitars must also accept that this excludes young people who find cathedral choirs or regular worship in their local church fresh and exciting.

'Anyone tempted to assume that youth worship is always fresh and exciting because it involves guitars must also accept that this excludes young people who find cathedral choirs or regular worship in their local church fresh and exciting.'

Spring 1999 saw Time of Our Lives, an enormous youth event organized by the Church of England. People came from all over England for a weekend which climaxed in a garden party at Lambeth Palace. On the Saturday evening there was a choice of services, all of which were well-attended and well-received: a rave service in Southwark Cathedral, modern praise at St Paul's and meditative style in Westminster Abbey. Examples of these types of worship can also be found at a local level and not just nationally. There is no single way of doing youth worship.

We might also expect youth worship to be more optimistic and active and enthusiastic than other forms of worship because young people themselves are more optimistic, active, enthusiastic. It might sometimes be true. However, there are other young people who are not like this, who just want the world to leave them alone, who are lethargic and weary, sometimes for good reasons. Youth worship need not always be bouncy and optimistic, any more than any worship need be. Young people, like everyone else, have problems and needs and fears. Worship which does not allow room for these is incomplete.

Youth worship is simply about young people worshipping God, nothing more and nothing less. It can be emotional or dull, disorganized or overly planned, too long or too short, just like any act of worship. And just like any act of worship, thank God, it can be redeemed and made glorious by the presence of the Trinity within us and within our shared worship.

THINKING IT THROUGH

1. Where do you worship God? Think of three things you've done this week which cause God to smile.

2. How easy do you find it to worship with other people? What is the cost of worshipping together? What is the cost of never worshipping together?
3. Do you find it easier to be close to God in the stillness of the moment or in the busyness of life? How could you get better at whichever you find harder?
4. Does youth worship exist? What shapes it? What are its weaknesses?
5. Think of the most amazing act of worship you've been to in the last three months (or year). What made it so brilliant?
6. Worship is life and life is worship. Discuss . . .

WHAT IS WORSHIP?

Since worship is both about what we do in church (or in any building, or the open air) and what we do every day in our everyday lives, worship works best when both are integrated. The last evening at Basecamp saw a Communion service. Because we had all been together for a fortnight, because we knew that the community was about to break up and we were all to return home, the atmosphere was intense and focused. It was an amazing service, so together and so united. We had prayed together and praised God together and lived together. Worship is about what we say and about what we do.

When we live as Christians, we see God at work in the world all around us. We don't leave worship behind with the hymn books at the church door – we take it with us as part of our new, transformed nature. How we live in the world can be about explicit Christian work, about being a worship leader or a missionary or a priest. It can also be about living out our lives in non-Christian work, like being an IT technician or a chef or working in a supermarket.

But it's not just about what hat we wear. It's also about who we are under the hat, about the way we deal with the people we live with and the way we relate to our friends and the way we relate to the

world. And who we are under the hat is a beloved child of God, called to love others into wholeness. We have the strength and courage to do that because, through praise and prayer, we remember who God is, who it is who is calling us to live in the world, to live our lives to his glory. And that praise and that living is worship. You cannot divide them for they are one. We say what we believe by what we do – and we live lives that are worship. That unity, the whole of our lives, is worship.

WHAT IS WORSHIP?

TAKING IT FURTHER

R. Bell, *Velvet Elvis*, Zondervan, 2005.

S. Conway and D. Stancliffe, *Living the Eucharist*, Darton, Longman & Todd, 2001.

S. Cottrell, *I Thirst: The cross – The great triumph of love*. Zondervan, 2004.

R. Giles, *Creating Uncommon Worship*, Canterbury Press, 2004.

S. Savage, S. Collins-Mayo, B. Mayo and G. Cray, *Making Sense of Generation Y: The world view of 15- to 25-year-olds*, Church House Publishing, 2006.

P. Ward, *Liquid Church*, Paternoster Press, 2002.

2 THE PLACE OF MUSIC IN WORSHIP

Helen Williams-Carter

> If music be the food of love, play on.
>
> William Shakespeare, *Twelfth Night*

INTRODUCTION

This chapter looks at the place music has in worship for young people, and the importance that is placed on music and corporate singing to God, on offering praise and worship, in the Bible.

This chapter considers the following questions:

- Is corporate singing outdated?
- Are we so hung up on the need to sing that we have lost the point of worship?

It is impossible within the limitations of a sole chapter to explore fully all the issues arising from such a subjective topic. Here, I present an overview of the subject based on personal experience and research with young people.

Drawing on the principle that God made us and knows how to connect with us, the underlying theme resounding throughout this chapter is that we sing songs of worship to God because we love him and he loves us.

THE ISSUE

Most music outside the Church is for background use, or individual appreciation, but always for personal gratification. You wouldn't choose to zone yourself into music that you didn't like – and with so much choice why should you?

This is where the Church seems to come up against what society is saying. In Church, music is not for our personal gratification, but to offer glory and praise to God our Father. While society has become introverted in its music appreciation, in church we still emphasize the importance of practising corporate worship, joining in acts of corporate singing, as we offer our praise to God as generations before us have. This can jar with young people, who have little or no other experience of corporate singing apart from the badly mumbled hymns on a Sunday morning, which do not often sound that worshipful!

So why do we continue to make these strangled sounds week in week out? Is it some sort of self-punishment? Have many of us got so hung up on the need to sing the hymns that we like, and have always sung, that we have lost the point of worship?

'Why do we continue to make these strangled sounds week in week out? Is it some sort of self-punishment? Have many of us got so hung up on the need to sing the hymns that we like, and have always sung, that we have lost the point of worship?'

THEORY AND BACKGROUND: The role of music in worship

Music has a powerful effect on human experience; it transcends our understanding and appeals to our intuitive nature. This being the case, it is not surprising that music has played an important role in worship in biblical communities and in today's society. It has been used as a way of approaching the mystery of God and expressing the joy of his presence.

Music in the Bible

We can look back through the Bible and see the importance that was placed on music and corporate singing to God, offering praise and worship. In Exodus 15, we read the song that Moses and the Israelites sang, after God helped them to escape from the Egyptians across the Red Sea. The Psalms are a collection of musical contributions and have been sung throughout the centuries, offering words and songs of praise to God in the trials and glories of life. In the New Testament, Jesus and his disciples sang together at the end of the Last Supper (Matthew 26.30).

As Paul instructs the New Testament churches:

> Let the word of Christ dwell in you richly; teach and admonish one another in all wisdom; and with gratitude in your hearts as you sing psalms, hymns, and spiritual songs to God. And whatever you do, whether in word or deed, do everything in the name of the Lord Jesus, giving thanks to God the Father through him.
>
> Colossians 3.16, 17

Worship is not simply a human activity on earth. In heaven, God's whole creation, humans and angels, praise and worship him (Revelation 4; 5; 7; 15).

'Worship is not simply a human activity on earth. In heaven, God's whole creation, humans and angels, praise and worship him.'

Music and song have continued to play important roles for God's people, in communities and society as a whole, from biblical times to the present day. Contemporary culture and modern technologies bring new possibilities, and new challenges, to the music ministry of the Church.

Music in contemporary culture

People's lives are surrounded by music: television, radio, personal CD players and mp3s, background music in shops and on computer games. Computer downloading of music has made the industry bigger than ever before.

Music in youth worship

The mistake that is often made is to think that all young people like the same style of worship: this is not the case, just as not all young people like the same style of music, clothing or pastimes. There are mainstream styles, which a lot of young people would find acceptable, and there are the smaller groups of select styles. And so it is with church worship. There is what is seen as the mainstream contemporary worship for young people, which has become known as 'Soul Survivor style worship', but this is not the be all and end all of youth worship.

'The mistake that is often made is to think that all young people like the same style of worship: this is not the case, just as not all young people like the same style of music, clothing or pastime.'

Why do thousands of young people make the pilgrimage to Taizé every year? This is certainly not what we affectionately class as youth worship: sitting on the ground in silent church services three times a day, singing chants repeatedly in foreign languages. But Taizé grips them, and thousands of young people feel the pull to return year after year. The whole place is enfolded in a prayerful spirit of worship, and offers a chance and space to connect with God, in a way not always offered in regular Sunday services. One young person told me that it is the 'simplicity of the unadulterated, unaccompanied human voice, offering simple words of praise, which is often overlooked', that helps him connect to God.

Then there are the big youth-focused worship events put on across the country. Manchester and Liverpool each host one of the biggest regular Christian youth gatherings in the country, SPACE, with over a thousand young people attending the monthly events, from all different walks of life – Christians from different denominations and non-Christians too. The SPACE events offer a range of top Christian artists and bands in various styles for the audience to enjoy. The evening ends with a time of corporate worship, where the words are displayed and young people have the opportunity to join in if they choose. While all the performers on stage are Christian, as is the majority of music they perform, the young people interviewed did not see this as worship, as they were passive participants in the act. One young person expressed it like this:

> Jumping around, dancing and having a laugh with my friends, is all music appreciation, but I'm not at that moment in time worshipping God, that comes later on in the evening.

But when the audience are given the opportunity to join in and worship, the mood changes across the whole theatre. The focus shifts from the band to

God, hands are raised in adoration of the Father, and words are sung with love to God.

Contemporary secular music is ever changing and developing, with new songs and styles released daily. If we are to use secular music in youth meetings the music needs to be of that moment, or it won't engage with young people's culture any more than a piece of classical music would. There is a vast range of music in the secular market, music that tackles issues going on around the world and in people's lives: war, famine, love, self-image, relationships. Music is a medium that young people know how to engage with, although you may not have realized its full potential for exploring different styles of worship.

Many youth groups use music tracks, not for corporate singing, as would instinctively be associated with music and worship, but as reflective pieces used in times of prayer to get into the hearts of young people, to help them offer prayers to God about their real-life situations, and to challenge young people's views on the world around them. For some young people this is a very powerful experience, where their culture meets biblical culture and God is found. (Some resources which suggest ways of using contemporary music in youth groups are listed on page 24.)

NEED TO KNOW: Is there a right or wrong style of youth worship?

Teenage years are full of changes, pressures and self-consciousness; no one wants to be seen as different from their peers. Big corporate worship events offer great experiences to engage with God in a place where anonymity can be found, where you don't feel different because you are a Christian, as the self-conscious individual is swallowed up by the sea of worshippers. Such opportunities are rarely the case in Sunday worship at the home church. Young people often struggle to fully engage, even if they enjoy the music. In a time when the music industry is massive and involved in every area of society, young people are engaging with God through new technologies.

The Bible gives no norms for worship style: they varied according to place and culture. So surely we should be extremely careful about expressing our judgements as to whether any particular style of worship is 'right' or 'wrong'.

In churches across the country some prefer their worship to be offered with choirs, processions, vestments and in liturgical forms. Others, however, like it simple with lots of participation, hearty singing and the raising of hands in adoration; both styles, and everything that falls in between, are correct – according to the needs of the worshippers. Temperament and culture are important considerations.

Young people, with their restless energy, will travel to experience different worship styles, and through these varied experiences are learning to worship. Even so, many put up with what to them is 'outdated' Sunday singing in church, though they recognize it is worship, and that is what is important.

'Many put up with what to them is "outdated" Sunday singing in church, though they recognize it is worship, and that is what is important.'

CASE STUDIES

A young gifted musician, who regularly played in a church music group, enjoyed playing the modern, more lively songs rather than the traditional hymns and felt that this was worship. Having been exposed to different environments and styles of worship, he experienced a taste of what worship was really about – an encounter of the heart with God. His concept of what constituted worship changed from seeing it as just playing and singing in the music group to realizing that it was more about actively seeking God and leading others, through the medium of music, whatever the style. As a result, for this young person, traditional hymns have been given a new lease of life: the words now have meaning as they are being sung to God.

Another young person expressed their attitude towards music like this:

> In times outside of the lively youth group and corporate worship events, young people are engaging in personal and private worship. Walking along the street or in the privacy of their own bedroom, worship music from a CD or MP3 is entering through their ears and

> affecting their hearts. Music is such a good way to switch out of busy situations and switch to God. MP3 makes it all easier and more discreet.

And finally a comment from another young person:

> Music is SO important in my life; it's the main way I connect with God. I feel it is really important that people experience God in a way that best works for them, and then they can relate this into their everyday experiences.

THINKING IT THROUGH

1. Which has more impact on the quality of worship for you, words or music?
2. Do you feel more comfortable engaging with God through corporate or individual worship times?
3. Have you had the opportunity to experience different styles of music in worship? Which style helps you engage with the heart of God most naturally?
4. Does your church offer opportunities to experience differing styles of music in worship? How can these opportunities be improved upon?
5. How can you use contemporary music in worship with young people with whom you work?

THE PLACE OF MUSIC IN WORSHIP

SUMMARY

Having started with the Bible and looked at worship through the years, the advancements of technology and explosion of differing cultures, it is clear that there has never been and never will be one set style of music for worship. We live in an ever-growing pick-and-mix culture, where no set style fits all but many styles can attract for differing reasons. However, there will always be one set focus and purpose for our worship, to offer our love in songs of praise to God our Father.

Surely worship is not only about the music, music is an aid; and it is not about singing someone else's words of praise, again an aid; it should be about what is in your heart being expressed to God. Music transcends all human thought and connects with God; God made us and he knows how to connect with us.

Matt Redman's song 'When the music fades' reminds us that it is not about how much technology a church possesses, or how many people are in the music group; it is about offering 'something that's of worth', that will bless God.[1] We worship because we love God, and corporate worship encourages and lifts our spirits as we, and others, offer the joys of our hearts to God.

We are all individuals and no two people will have the same experience in worship; God made us unique and connects uniquely with each and every one of us. Young people, in fact all of us, need to have opportunities to experience different styles of worship in order to have a true worship encounter with God. When, for each individual, the music seems to interact with the songs of the angels, and all of creation is singing praise to God; when this happens we experience the true heart of worship.

Many people in church need to experience the heart of worship, and realize that they too can engage in a way that is not their chosen style (it may even mean giving youth worship a chance!). It is more about being in an environment conducive to connecting and engaging with God than the style in which this is offered.

'If music be the food of love, play on.' Worship is our love response to Jesus, and love cannot be bound with rules and regulations.

THE PLACE OF MUSIC IN WORSHIP

TAKING IT FURTHER

The following resources are recommended for those who wish to explore the subject further.

S. Adams and R. Adams, *Music to Move the Soul*, Authentic Media Publishing, 2003.

P. Angier, *Changing Youth Worship*, Church House Publishing, 1997.

Andy Flannagan, *Distinctive Worship*, Authentic Media Publishing, 2004.

L. Giglio, *The Air I Breathe (Worship as a Way of Life)*, Kingsway, 2003.

Matt Redman, 'When the music fades', *Intimacy – Track 8: The heart of worship*. Survivor Records, 1998.
www.heartofworship.com/

3 WORD OF LIFE? PRAYER AND WORD IN WORK WITH YOUNG PEOPLE

Diane J. Craven

The Word became flesh and lived among us.

John 1.14

INTRODUCTION

Describing an experience in an art gallery where the visitors became participants in the exhibit, Mike Riddell and others reflect on a desire for worship that has a similar level of engagement and where the outcomes are not restricted but dependent on those involved. 'Active participation with open-ended interpretation. Room to move physically and cognitively.'[1] It is a vision that might equally well apply to our prayer practices and to the ways in which we seek to engage with the word of God in work with young people.

What we do in the realms of prayer and word needs to reflect these twin principles of engagement (rather than entertainment) and the possibility of interpretation that opens up possibilities for future study and engagement rather than closing them down. It is also important to remember that young people are not empty vessels but bring with them their own experience, their encounters with God, their grasp of the spiritual, their various commitments and their connections to the cultures to which they belong. All of these can be carriers of the revelation of God, albeit at times in oblique ways. If word

'Young people are not empty vessels but bring with them their own experience, their encounters with God, their grasp of the spiritual, their various commitments and their connections to the cultures to which they belong. All of these can be carriers of the revelation of God, albeit at times in oblique ways.'

and prayer are to become important sustaining influences, then they have to be seen as opportunities for active participation, involving our whole lives and our whole selves. There is nothing, therefore, that is 'off-limits' if we hold to the fact that the gospel is robust enough to speak with power and to affect each and every generation.

In the Incarnation Christ inhabited our space and moved around in it, 'bone of our bone and flesh of our flesh'.[2] It is perhaps the traditional Christian doctrine of the Incarnation together with a grasp of liturgy and of contemplative practices that can offer us a useful framework within which to operate. The revelation of God in Christ was not expressed as abstraction, somehow removed from the harsh realities of daily living. Instead, the revelation of God is made known in human flesh with all its frailties and weakness as well as its potential. Otherwise there is nothing that the gospel can speak into the mess of everyday lives and the chaos which many of us live in, whether external or internal.

Today, prayer and the word need to be interpreted afresh for this generation in order that they become not constraining forces but are instead that which we move around in to make new meanings for our day and our situation. This means that we need to find new ways of encouraging the engagement of young people with Scripture, without assuming that Scripture, or how we view it, automatically has authority to speak into the lives of young people. The days of linear narrative and of meta-narrative are long gone and today's postmoderns are highly suspicious of anything that resembles or is dependent on external authority. In such a climate, the weight of the book can be seen as oppressive and restrictive, and the playful and ironic become important methods of response and enquiry. This does not mean, however, that we can be sloppy in our own exegesis or hermeneutics, or that we can shy away from the difficult stuff. Nor does it mean that we do not encourage young people to work at finding their way in terms of approaches to the Bible or to prayer. Young people (and indeed adults) today are much more likely to engage with prayer and the Bible by being drawn in to puzzle over interpretation, or to respond to apparently

'Prayer and the word need to be interpreted afresh for this generation'

clashing ideas, or to wonder over story or poetry, or by being startled that something written so long ago can still express aspects of human behaviour and emotion with amazing clarity. They need to be taken seriously and to be given the tools with which to dig into prayer and the Bible for themselves.

THE ISSUE

It is by now a frequent assertion that we are no longer in a word-based culture, but a visual one. The information we take in, we take in primarily through the visual sense and through the sense impressions of images in flux or counterpoint.

However, simply to say we are in a visual culture would seem to be missing something important, namely the sense of the spiritual that is so prevalent in our times, judging by the numbers of book dedicated to the topic in any bookshop today. One of the key things that makes Christian spirituality distinctive is that it is patterned on the way of Christ rather than based on 'feel-good' experiences. Word and prayer are set against a backdrop of a desire for the spiritual, for what is inexplicable or 'beyond', and the desire to express belief in physical and symbolic ways. As Mike Riddell has commented: 'Post-modern times are *tactile, symbolic and image-based*.'[3]

'Word and prayer are set against a backdrop of a desire for the spiritual, for what is inexplicable or "beyond", and the desire to express belief in physical and symbolic ways.'

In today's culture where everything is 'up for grabs' and where nothing and everything can be seen as holy, we witness in particular ways a deep human desire to seek out and to touch the unknown. The importance of what Beaudoin calls 'sacramentals', which he describes as 'miniature, personal signs of God's grace in the world', is particularly pertinent in this context.[4] Those who work with young people have a crucially important role to play in discovering and interpreting what personal signs of God's grace already exist in the lives of young people. It is also their task do the work of helping

'Those who work with young people have a crucially important role to play in discovering and interpreting what personal signs of God's grace already exist in the lives of young people.'

young people connect their lives and the word of God through symbols and symbolic objects and actions and by so doing to enable young people to experience the holiness of God as both immanent and transcendent.

THEORY AND BACKGROUND

> We declare to you what was from the beginning, what we have heard, what we have seen with our eyes, what we have looked at and touched with our hands, concerning the word of life – this life was revealed, and we have seen it and testify to it, and declare to you the eternal life that was with the Father and was revealed to us.
>
> 1 John 1.1–2

There is an immediacy in these words from 1 John which goes straight to the heart of the contemporary quest for authenticity, for the inexplicable to be revealed in ways that we can touch and handle, and for felt experience – experience which touches, challenges, seizes our imaginations, makes us puzzle and wonder, moves us and maybe even changes us. There is a reality here (this life) which the words are reaching after but which just manages to elude being pinned down in a definition. We saw it, we were there, we witnessed it, we knew it was true – didn't we? And how did we know? Certainly not by simply being told it was a good thing! This richly evocative passage reminds us above all that we are physical beings and that what we know of God is mediated to us in a variety of ways including through what we hear, see, gaze upon, touch and handle. It reminds us, too, that God speaks to us supremely in the Incarnation, through which matter, flesh, the body is validated. God is indeed 'bone of our bone and flesh of our flesh'.

'God speaks to us supremely in the Incarnation, through which matter, flesh, the body is validated.'

It is no accident that the Scriptures are full of wordplay, for God is a God who speaks in both direct and ambiguous ways. God's word calls worlds into being, the voice of God calls a people, God speaks through the prophets, through the covenant – the word of promise – and 'in these last days he has spoken to us by a Son . . .' (Hebrews 1.2) who is God's self-communication embodied. And even then what God has to say is not always immediately understood. Young people have a great deal to teach adults about the God who is sometimes very present and then at other times seems to have disappeared, and about the authenticity that tells it like it is rather than covering over the experience of the absence of God and pretending that the reality is different. And perhaps teenagers are closer than many adults to the rawness of the ups and downs of relationships.

Like a precious gift, the true meaning and value of God's presence with us accrues over time, within the context of ongoing relationship. Like the giving of one self to another within a relationship, God gifts us with the meaning of his own nature – his own self – once and for all in Christ but also in ongoing ways, for there are to be aspects of this gift which we continue to peel back, uncovering layer after layer of mystery. The meaning of God's self-revelation in Christ also continues to unfold for us as we play our part in dialogue with the story of that revelation and continue to puzzle over and to experience how that meaning is contained for us in Scripture and in sacrament. God's

'The meaning of God's self-revelation in Christ also continues to unfold for us as we play our part in dialogue with the story of that revelation and continue to puzzle over and to experience how that meaning is contained for us in Scripture and in sacrament.'

validation of created matter, our flesh, our life lived in the body becomes important then for how we take hold of God's self-revelation. It is through the body that God speaks: 'The basic experience of life that each one of us has is the first and fundamental word that God speaks to us.'[5] It becomes vital then that both life experience and the tactile, sensory and physical are seen as part of our encounter with the Bible and part of our prayer life and the way that we express things to God.

As Pete Ward has remarked, 'Ritual helps us to make the transition from the ordinary to the transcendent and back again.'[6] Ritual can assist us in doing the work of connecting experience – the stuff of our own lives – with the word of God. It can also assist us in recognizing the presence of God within the fabric of our day-to-day living. More than this, when it is working as it should, ritual does not allow us to forget our connection to the world and to each other. Nor should it allow us to forget the intimate connectedness of our story and God's story: 'what we have looked at and touched with our hands, concerning the word of life' (1 John 1.1). What contemporary spiritual enquiry and expression seem to indicate is that physical approaches to text engage people by showing us that it is possible to understand text as a dynamic and living thing – something we do and to which we respond with the whole of ourselves, body included!

'Ritual can assist us in doing the work of connecting experience – the stuff of our own lives – with the word of God.'

In an experience of doing Celtic Body Prayer (expressing the Lord's Prayer through simple set movements), one young person said:

> I always thought the Lord's Prayer was something that you . . . like . . . said with your eyes shut and that. When we did it with movement, at first, I thought this is going to be a bit, like, weird, but when we did it, it made me think about how big the world is and that we are small really but . . . well . . . God is still bothered about us.

In another experience, this time using stones in a symbolic way to help young people engage with the idea of confession and letting go of the burdens we hold on to, one participant said: 'When I dropped the stone into the water, I really felt like I was letting go of being angry and it really helped.' This is not to say that every time we worship we need to use such actions or symbols simply because they seem like a good, catchy idea to try out. Young people are highly adept at spotting gimmicks and things that don't spring from an authentic experience that the leader has made his or her own and is sharing. When being encouraged (yet again) to express their prayer with uncreative involvement of a stone, one young person was heard to mutter in a worship gathering: 'Not *another* prayer thing to do with a stone – it's a stone, big deal!' It isn't enough to simply include objects just for the sake of it and without doing the work of considering the purpose they serve, the particular reasons for using them now and in this context and the meaning they are intended to carry.

NEED TO KNOW

The concept of dialogue is of primary importance in our consideration of the interchange between adults and young people. It may also provide us with a 'way in' to understanding the ways in which theology shapes practice (and vice versa) and the two-way exchange between experience and revelation.

It is vital that those who work with young people are attentive to culture as well as to the gospel. That means that we need to take seriously the 'signals of transcendence' that are being exhibited in and through the culture of which we are a part.[7] This might include, for example:

- responses to issues in the news which reveal young people's take on current matters of local or global concern;
- situations and experiences that young people talk about which they do not find it easy to explain (or which defy explanation altogether), including life experiences both good and bad, such as encountering death, and what some call 'spooky experiences' – unexplained mystery or, for some, encounters with the occult;
- experiences of aloneness or moments of joy;
- falling in and out of love;

and the feeling of being in touch with life and the world.

We need to work at understanding the messages they are articulating and then to begin to determine what tools are necessary – for us as much as for young people – to evaluate and critique culture and to allow the gospel to come under the scrutiny of culture. Only then should we think how to make these tools available to the young people with whom we work and to whom we minister. It is important too that young people themselves set the agenda shaped by what is of concern to them, rather than well-meaning adults setting up discussions on 'what the Bible has to say about . . .' with their own agenda shaping the matters under discussion. Boundaries and safe space are also important for this kind of exchange to take place.

There is also a task to do in creating sacramentals for our times and in learning how to work with these in prayer, Bible reflection and worship. This may involve words but equally might involve images or symbolic objects as appropriate.

'There is also a task to do in creating sacramentals for our times and in learning how to work with these in prayer, Bible reflection and worship.'

We need to learn how to do wordplay! This involves discovering ways of engaging in dialogue between word and culture; of seeing the word in culture, of challenging culture. It requires that we become open to a variety of interpretations and discover text as a space in which to move. It means time set aside to do our research of the cultures young people inhabit, taking seriously the concerns, commitments and interests to which popular culture with all its fashions, fads and crazes bears witness. Film, music and lyrics, fashion, magazines and newspapers are all rich sources.

It means time set aside to hear the stories young people wish to tell – to listen to these stories and to respect their integrity and the specific cultures in which these stories have taken root.

It means being prepared to interpret the signs of the times in the light of the word *and* being prepared to put our own commitments and values under scrutiny, since transformation is a two-way activity.

CASE STUDY: Prayer practice based on the Ignatian tradition

The Ignatian practice of the *Examen* brings everyday life and word into dialogue and enables those who practise it to begin to see the patterning of life as the locus for revelation. The Spiritual Exercises of St Ignatius begin with a recommendation to practise the *Examen*, which is based on the belief that God speaks to us through the pattern of what he called 'consolation' and 'desolation'. We might understand 'consolation' to be all that connects us to our selves to others to the world and to God; and its converse, 'desolation', as all that disconnects us from these things.

The practice is very simple and requires just some space and a context conducive to reflecting on the day (or a longer period of time). A candle is lit as a symbol of God's illuminating presence and two questions are reflected upon: For what am I most grateful? For what am I least grateful? Or putting it another way: What has brought me life today? What has made life drain from me? Or: What was today's high point? What was today's low point? The practice can be done individually or in a small group where individuals can decide how much detail they wish to share.

An example of this practice as used in a youth group involved young people in creating a time line on large sheets of paper on which they marked the key events in their lives to date and alongside this they marked the points where they had felt the presence of God and the places where it seemed that God was absent. (Within a group this can be done individually or as an interactive activity, depending on the nature of the group and the levels of trust within it.) Psalm 139 provided a Scripture focus and verses of the Psalm together with other relevant verses of Scripture were printed out on slips of paper which the young people then placed at strategic points on their life map(s). Candles could also be placed on the map to show where God's revelation was felt/seen/experienced most keenly. A pile of cards was provided which had written on them words and phrases to express various ways of encountering God, such as friends, family, school, Bible, prayer, church, being alone, and some blank cards for other alternatives that the young people wanted to include. The cards were then also placed on the time line at strategic points to represent where they had encountered God at various times.

The young people wrote on one coloured Post-it note what they were thankful for and on a different-coloured Post-it, a question or a regret, or something that would have been a help to them that wasn't there at the time. There was then some group reflection on the pattern of our lives and the ways in which we could see – looking back on it – the work of God in our lives in both good and difficult times and what had helped us or hindered us in encountering God in all these times. Without doubt, being able to see this spread out on the floor and the act of engaging in creating it helped the group in their consideration of the presence (or absence) of God throughout their lives and stimulated reflection throughout the process of creating the time line.

There was some silence (though open prayer could have been equally appropriate) to consider what we wished to thank God for and to pray for others and the situations of their lives. Then verses of Psalm 139 were read over an extract from 'Mad World'[8] played on CD (which took a fair amount of practice by the leader!) and a final prayer was said, using the words: 'You are made, known and loved by God.' These words were written on cards that the young people took away with them and which they were encouraged to reflect on during the week using them as a kind of mantra.

THINKING IT THROUGH

1. What enables you to draw near, to touch God in worship, Bible study or prayer? Have you found space for these experiences within your regular diet of worship in your church?

   In thinking about how to apply the practice of prayer or Bible reflection with young people, we might consider how the riches of our liturgical tradition can be of help in thinking through practice of prayer and Bible reflection or study. Examples linked to this include, for example, thinking about the person of Christ through the changing story of the Church year; seasons and their images and symbols; times of thinking through our responsibility to the world and to creation, and times for setting our own lives in order; adapting Lenten practices; thinking through the meaning of the Cross in a world obsessed by celebrity, beauty, status and money; reflecting on the meaning of the Incarnation in the midst of the tinsel and Santas of popular culture.

2. Linked to this is the possibility of exploring some traditional iconography and setting these images alongside media images, for example of famous faces. What do the images say to us about God and about human beings? Which ones are compelling and why? Which ones are comfortable and which ones are disturbing and why? Similarly, a group might explore faces of Jesus or look at how Jesus is presented in various traditional images and in more recent examples. What difference is made to our understanding of God if we look at an image of a black Christ or a Christ from another culture?

   As image is so important to young people, we should be equipping them to evaluate and challenge some of the images that surround them.

3. Think through a typical service in your church – individually or in a group setting. What aspects of it appeal to the senses of hearing, seeing, tasting, touching or smelling? When might everyday objects, images or experiences be or become carriers of God's revelation?
4. Think about a time when you recall being sustained by the word of God or by prayer. Where did you as an adult last have the opportunity to reflect on the word of God?
5. Think about your own prayer practice. What practices of prayer have helped you in your Christian journey? Have different practices helped you at different times?
6. If you are a leader of a church or a youth group, where do you find spaces and opportunities to explore alternative ways in to the word of God which can support and extend what you already find helpful?
7. How might you give young people a rich diet of prayer practices which can provide them with resources to draw on at different times in their lives?
8. What have you located in your own life as a 'sacramental'? Can these sacramentals be reinterpreted with and for young people today? How might you work with the sacramentals that resonate with young people?

WORD OF LIFE? PRAYER AND WORD IN WORK WITH YOUNG PEOPLE

SUMMARY

It is all too easy to find ourselves over emphasizing cultural relevance at the expense of integrity. In the face of the pressures faced by young people today, reflective practices of prayer and biblical engagement can be a means of giving them a practice which can provide lasting nourishment. We are doing young people a great disservice if we deny them experiences in prayer and word which resonate with their experience and fire their imaginations. And these things, drawn from disparate sources (not all of them overtly 'spiritual') and from the maelstrom of daily life, are sacramentals for our day – 'God with us' – given symbolic expression and validating for us the meaning of life lived in the body. As Mike Riddell has aptly observed: 'the nature of creation is such that any element of it may become a symbol . . . a mediator of the presence and activity of God'.[9] It is the job of all who minister in the Church to find those sacramentals which best make the eternal word flesh for the people of God in this culture and this time.

WORD OF LIFE? PRAYER AND WORD IN WORK WITH YOUNG PEOPLE

This is by no means an exhaustive list but it does provide a mix of theory, theology and praxis.

Jenny Baker, *Transforming Prayer*, Spring Harvest, 2004.

Jenny Baker and Moya Ratnayake, *Tune In, Chill Out: Using contemplative prayer in youth work* (includes a CD-ROM with music, meditations, visual and written material), Christian Education, 2004. A rich resource of ideas including centring prayer and prayer practices from a variety of traditions.

Jonny Baker and Doug Gay, with Jenny Brown, *Alternative Worship*, SPCK, 2003.

Peter L. Berger, *A Rumour of Angels*, Penguin, 1969.

Walter Brueggemann, *The Bible and Post-Modern Imagination: Texts under negotiation*, Fortress, 1993.

Kenda Creasy Dean, Chap Clark and Dave Rahn (eds), *Starting Right: Thinking theologically about youth ministry*, Zondervan, 2001.

Tim E. Dearborn and Scott Coll (eds), *Worship at the Next Level: Insight from contemporary voices*, Baker Books, 2004.

Andy Flannagan, *Distinctive Worship*, Authentic Media Publishing, 2004.

Tony Jones, *Soul Shaper: Exploring spirituality and contemplative practices in youth ministry*, Zondervan, 2004.

John M. Sweeney, *Praying with Our Hands: 21 practices of embodied prayer from the world's spiritual traditions*, Wild Goose Publications, 2000.

Sue Wallace, *Multi-Sensory Prayer*, Scripture Union, 2000.

Sue Wallace, *Multi-Sensory Church*, Scripture Union, 2002.

Pete Ward (ed.), *The Rite Stuff*, Bible Reading Fellowship, 2004.

Dick Westley, *A Theology of Presence*, Twenty-Third Publications, 1998.

Walter Wink, *Transforming Bible Study*, Abingdon Press, 1989.

USPG have produced a pack called *The Christ We Share*, which is a starting point for images of Christ.

You might also like to look at the rejesus web site, which contains ideas for prayer and is a good source of visual material to reflect on and sometimes to puzzle over with young people. www.rejesus.co.uk

Life Coach Bruce Stanley has produced sets of cards which contain creative ways in to prayer and reflection. www.onearthasinheaven.co.uk carries details of the cards and information about how to order them.

A simple guide to using the *Examen* can be found in:
Dennis Linn, Sheila Fabricant Linn and Matthew Linn, *Sleeping with Bread: Holding what gives you life*, Paulist Press, 1995.

CREATIVE APPROACHES TO LITURGY

SECTION 2

In this section you will find a triplet of chapters that guide your thinking through engaging young people with existing liturgy. This might be the point at which you and your church enter the discussion of engaging young people in worship, as the tradition of your church meets the new culture.

First, Tim Sledge looks at the place that rites and rituals have in today's worshipping communities and offers some insightful reflections on the role they have in young people's lives. Jean Kerr then suggests ways of encouraging young people to engage creatively with liturgy within the context of a traditional church service. Finally in this section, Susie Mapledoram tackles the problematic issue of all-age worship and considers how to make it truly appealing to all ages, including young people.

4 RITES AND RITUALS IN WORSHIP

Tim Sledge

INTRODUCTION

'So what is your most memorable worship experience?' The question was posed to a group of teenagers. Some of them were part of the local church, others were 'fringe church' – they enjoyed meeting in a discussion group, but mainstream church was a struggle for them.

Their answers[1] were interesting and had an important bearing both on my approach to leading worship with young people and to this chapter:

> 'I remember my nephew's baptism – it was really special. Good that everyone was together and the baptism ceremony seemed like a really big deal to the parents,' said one.
>
> 'I remember this time when we got together for a dawn service on Easter Day overlooking the reservoir! It was amazing!' said another.
>
> And another: 'I know you are going to think I am weird, but we had this service in church on Good Friday – the Tenebrae – it was really spooky and moody but I really felt God. The music, the darkness, the candles was amazing.'

The next question: 'What are the big turn-offs for you in a worship service?' The replies came thick and fast! 'Action songs, boring prayers, sermons not relevant to our age, not knowing the songs or hymns, long sermons, pointless life stories.'

These replies, I believe, speak loudly of the need to make connections with people through relationships and what is going on in worship. In the first set of answers, the ritual and special events are making a connection – as is the environment, the sense of the special, the numinous. There is a 'wow' factor, and also recognition of the integrity of what is happening. In the second set of answers, we see a list of dislikes and a degree of anger rooted in a feeling that the Church is making no connection with their lives – and like many people of all ages, they crave that connection.

The connection which these young people spoke of is coming through what the Church would call its rites and rituals. Recognizing the impact and connection that many of the Church's existing rituals can and do make, this chapter will explore the value and potency of rituals, and will consider how many rituals exist in the lives of young people, and their importance. Two cases studies will show that, with a little bit of creativity, the Church already has plenty to offer young people through what already happens and argue that rites and rituals help young people to make a connection with the living God.[2]

THE ISSUE

Rites and ritual have often been treated with suspicion by those from different traditions within the Church. Many churches feel that rites and ritual (particularly those which are part of the Church's history) are irrelevant and would serve to alienate rather than engage young people. We will define rite and ritual below, but here it is important to recognize that all Church traditions have their own rites and rituals, even if it is something as simple as having a 'worship time' rather than the more traditional 'hymn sandwich'.

> **'All Church traditions have their own rites and rituals, even if it is something as simple as having a "worship time" rather than the more traditional "hymn sandwich".'**

But recent years have seen something of a sea change in attitudes. Many now acknowledge that rites and ritual have an important place in worship with young people, particularly as there is a natural link with young people's own culture, which is multi-sensory, full of symbols and icons of which young people are sophisticated interpreters. Because there is so much power and meaning in symbol and there are so many different ways to make connections, we have only begun to scratch the surface.

THEORY AND BACKGROUND

Let's begin by defining our terms.

What are rites and rituals?

A *rite* is a form of worship, the skeleton. It is a framework for *rituals*. We flesh and clothe the skeleton with appropriate dress – the rituals. As such, ritual gives rite life, meaning and identity. It is the expression within the framework. Rites of worship have been carefully woven together throughout history.

The most familiar rites of worship are the Eucharist or Holy Communion, baptism, funerals and weddings. Many freer styles of worship also have rites of 'Worship, Word and Ministry'. Rites have a sense of shape and flow about them. They also have within them significant rituals to add significance. For example, in a baptism service, the signing of the cross with Holy Oil, use of water and the giving and receiving of a candle are rituals to mark a significant point in life.

Rituals in the Church have developed over centuries and we have developed new rituals over time. For example, the recent Services for Healing and Wholeness provide rite and ritual to help people come to the wholeness of life, which Christ desires for every human being.

Rite and ritual in Scripture

The Scriptures are full of rites and rituals. Many of these stories of ritual speak powerfully of the faithfulness and presence of God. The Jewish rites of purification, for example in Leviticus, are not just rules and regulations, but rituals to mark change, from sinfulness to cleansing, from being an outsider to belonging. The ritual of the sacrifice in the story of Abraham and Isaac was a symbolic action through which God spoke. The burning bush on Mount Sinai was a symbol through which God spoke. In both of these examples, it is not the symbol that speaks, but God who speaks through the symbol. Jesus too reclothed rites and used the Passover meal at his last supper to be the first

'Through symbols God is made real and speaks often more loudly than the words could!'

meal of the new covenant. Through symbols God is made real and speaks often more loudly than the words could!

Rituals in the lives of young people

The lives of young people are full of rituals – from the first kiss to the first exam, from puberty to passing a driving test. Watch any news footage of young people receiving their A level and GCSE results. There is a ritual in how these are presented and how young people gather to celebrate and commiserate with each other.

Young people also make new rituals for themselves. When was the last time you observed a group of young people – their greetings, hairstyles and the way they behave in groups? It's worth engaging in. The recent trend of wearing wristbands to ally people to a certain issue such as poverty, racism and breast cancer is an example of a small and simple ritual which helps young people identify with others and demonstrate an allegiance.

'Young people also make new rituals for themselves. When was the last time you observed a group of young people – their greetings, hairstyles and the way they behave in groups?'

As ritual plays such a powerful and significant part in the lives of young people, it makes absolute sense to see how the ritual in the life of the Church can make connections with the ritual in the lives of young people.

'As ritual plays such a powerful and significant part in the lives of young people, it makes absolute sense to see how the ritual in the life of the Church can make connections with the ritual in the lives of young people.'

Recently during a Eucharist for young people, one teenager who had never seen robes used in worship asked what I was wearing and why. When this was explained her response was: 'Cool! This is something special isn't it?'

The fear of ritual

We are concerned about how our young people are formed and grow and we are therefore concerned about how ritual is used. One of these concerns is over understanding. Should we really be presenting something in worship which is not defined and which some adults themselves don't understand? This lack of understanding adds to the fear of ritual and we need to educate both adults and young people to know the importance of ritual. In response, I would say that I have never met anyone who fully understands both our rituals and the wonder and completeness of God. In a world that is constantly looking for meaning and answers, there is an increasing fascination with mystery. You only have to look at the increase of New Age shops or the quest for spiritual experience via Eastern religions and meditation. Most young people do not try to understand and rationalize but make connections through feelings and experience, and through these, glimpse something of the presence of God. This is not to say explanation, teaching and a growing understanding of the truths of the Christian faith are not fundamental, as is sharing the gospel with young people, but rather that in worship, ritual and experience are essential and not as fearful and 'dodgy' as some might think.

Ritual: caged or free-range?!

Young people long to be set free in worship: the capacity to play and explore and to wonder does not disappear in early childhood. Alongside this, as anyone with teenage children will know, go the agonies of wrestling with rules, which seem to control and restrict a teenage desire to break out! The tragedy is that the Church has often used ritual to control, like some sort of holding pen for stray and recalcitrant animals that need to be kept under control and under authority. I hope that the more creative use of ritual in worship will not be so used.

It can also be all too easy to hide behind our rituals. While everything around us changes, we think that if we hang onto our ancient traditions, dress them up even more, shout even louder, then maybe people will come back to the Church and to the faith. It was Sigmund Freud who said: 'The definition of insanity is doing the same thing over and over again expecting a different result.'[3] Much ritual is simply endless, thoughtless repetition and lacks life and integrity.

'Free-range' ritual demands more thought and creativity because young people need to be stimulated by a constant variety of image, sound and experience. There is always a challenge to the Church to be creative in finding connections, rather than finding one thing which works and sticking with it for eternity. For example, two different confessions: Both use a large cross, both involve placing sins onto a cross. One involves Post-it notes and the other nailing pieces of red ribbon to a cross. The ritual is similar, but the expression of it is different. We constantly need to keep variety in ritual with young people. Free-range teenagers are constantly looking for new experiences and expressions of faith and life.

'"Free-range" ritual demands more thought and creativity because young people need to be stimulated by a constant variety of image, sound and experience.'

Culture and ritual

We receive information in a whole variety of ways, and we learn in a variety of ways – through visual, symbolic, literal, aural cues as well as the more traditionally didactic ways we are more used to.[4]

The great strength of ritual and symbol is that they mean different things to different people. This is a wonderful opportunity for creativity in worship and if we could realize it, actually plays to our strengths. Young people respond to ambiguity rather than absolutes and need the space to explore and be challenged.

When I co-founded an alternative worship service in Huddersfield in the mid 1990s, we called it *Sanctuary: a safe place to meet with God*. By accident, we had stumbled across exactly what young people – especially young adults – were looking for, and that was the sense of space, of safety, of Sanctuary. In the worship services, we always had a space which was for nothing – space for space's sake. The general shape of the worship was to have a central worship space with large sheets hung between pillars onto which images were projected. In addition, all around the church were smaller zones where different themes of worship could be explored, or people could receive ministry, be silent and still, or noisy and active.[5] One of these zones was the 'chill-out' zone – sacred and safe space. What we found was that the space was always well used and became a key part of every act of worship which we created. What we began to realize was that sacred space, retreat, the safety and stillness of the cradling arms of God was one of the most precious and needed experiences to process all that was going on between the worshipper and God.

We also recognized that we were using the tradition of Christian rites and rituals as a living resource to draw from. As we developed worship services,[6] we began to see things from different traditions being used side by side and given fresh expression. Effective worship for young people involves learning from the riches of the Church tradition while making strong connections with the world of everyday culture, but giving young people the space and freedom to graze in open spaces of worship history and create their own.

'Effective worship for young people involves learning from the riches of the Church tradition while making strong connections with the world of everyday culture, but giving young people the space and freedom to graze in open spaces of worship history and create their own.'

Using rites and rituals moved us from a tradition of the *Menu du jour* with limited choice, to a wider buffet.[7] History was no longer dead and ritual old and tired, but rather history was seen as an archive with full freedom of access to all areas.

NEED TO KNOW: Connecting with rite and ritual

How rites and rituals connect with young people today will be different from area to area. Making the connections with young people's lives will mean listening to the styles, tastes, needs and expectations of young people as well as understanding some of their rituals. It will mean acknowledging the short shelf life of many of these styles. It means that some rituals may also have a short shelf life, but this shouldn't matter. Services and worship opportunities which were right five years ago might not be now. Teenagers grow out of clothes and fashions and fads, and are extraordinarily fickle with history. By responding to this we are being wise stewards of Christian worship history – always on the ball, and always seeking to renew in order that we can continue to make connections with young people in worship.

Ritual, like tradition, is a living organism. Rites and rituals also help to provide a sort of glue – like the handshake, like the recognized routines which are the framework for our day, such as the basics of cleaning teeth, the same seat on the bus to college and so on. They also hold church life together. Rites and rituals help create a context where people can meet God in the framework of the gospel. They can provide reference points helping us on our pilgrimage of life, rather than anchors, weighing us down to one place while the world flows by.

'Rites and rituals help create a context where people can meet God in the framework of the gospel. They can provide reference points helping us on our pilgrimage of life, rather than anchors, weighing us down to one place while the world flows by.'

Not all ritual needs to be religious. One of the key challenges for all worship is how it makes connections to daily life. Many symbols and rituals are based around food, music and dress, and places people go and meet. Symbols and ritual are the way young people form their identity. As we seek to lead young people in worship so they will seek their true identity as the adored children of God, we can use the common and the ordinary and everyday within the ritual of the Church and reclothe this to make sense today. For example, recently a group of clergy have reinterpreted the tradition of foot-washing on Maundy Thursday by cleaning people's shoes in the centre of Peterborough, as a ritual of service and love. The most fascinated, intrigued and touched by this process have been young people – who can't believe that we should do something for nothing, who want to have their shoes or trainers or rollerblades cleaned, and who respect what we are doing. Here is a ritual which they have to be involved with. You can't just watch someone's shoes being cleaned and get something out of it – much better to feel what its like to have them done for you.

As we have seen in recent years, when tragic events happen (e.g. the death of Diana, the Asian tsunami disaster) people often want to respond in symbolic ways, by doing rather than just saying. People also want to share in an act together – we all light candles or bring flowers or keep vigil. Ritual is a shared corporate act, which impacts on us individually.

Part of that doing and saying is about going somewhere. Makeshift shrines are created on roadsides and outside royal palaces. But there are a variety of shrines which have been so important to many over the years and are key places of going and doing for young people. Places such as Taizé, and Walsingham, Soul Survivor and Spring Harvest, New Wine and Soul in the City are all about going and doing and about the growing realization that the whole of creation is sacramental. They are also about going with others. In the words of Meister Eckhart, from the fourteenth century: 'Every moment God is giving birth to Jesus in all of creation.' The ritual of going somewhere and seeking God in the special place is increasingly important for young people – as is the creation of their own space. How many of our churches feel as if they are space owned for and by young people?

One of the reasons why people avoid the use of symbols and rituals in worship is that they don't realize what we have already. Or because what we use has lost its meaning and value.

Here are some suggestions for rethinking our use of rite and ritual in our work with young people:

- Try doing a sort of inventory of all the symbols you have in church with the young people. Are there any parallels in everyday life? Could we use these as well? For example, the font and cleansing lotions, hymnody and modern songs, communion and food, prayer and communication.
- How do we use the space?
- How can we use all the senses?
- Where do we meet?
- Explore new symbols and rituals – what do modern-day labels mean to us? How can these be used in worship?
- How do we use silence in our worship?
- Do we light candles and have images and activities to help us in our worship?
- What might we do to open a door on to God?
- Invite the young people to bring symbols which are important to them, and explore the church to see what speaks to them and why.

One way to begin to build worship in this style is with a group of people and a blank sheet of paper. It takes time, prayer, fellowship and freedom. It takes time to help young people have confidence in the rituals they are creating. Rituals must make connections, but we need to be aware that these connections will be different for different people. Worship like this does not come quickly or off the peg, but is bespoke and therefore takes longer.

CASE STUDY: Critical Mass

Recently in the Diocese of Peterborough, we staged Critical Mass. This was primarily aimed at the small numbers of young people in middle-of-the-road or more catholic parishes where worship often was making little connection with the lives of young people, and yet where they respected the rituals, even if they meant little to them.

We wanted to create a space for the Eucharist to live and speak to the lives of young people. Multimedia images, video cameras and still images were used, but the key symbols of word and sacrament maintained their prominence. There was a mixture of the contemporary and the more traditional. The Eucharistic Prayer was an authorized *Common Worship* prayer with a sung response, the readings were read and dramatized. There were processions, with people coming out of the body of Christ to contribute to the liturgy and then returning. There was discussion as we broke open the Scriptures together. After we had shared communion around the altar, we then shared pizzas and garlic bread. In short, a framework was provided and the young people built the liturgy around within it. It demonstrated the true meaning of liturgy – 'the work of the people' – rather than the work of experts in putting words together.

For many people there, it was the most powerful experience of worship they had been to. For many of the leaders, it gave them permission to try some more creative things in their own churches. It also showed that making connections in worship is about becoming active participants in connecting with the living God rather than being passive observers of a beautifully orchestrated and choreographed spectacle.

What we also observed was that the impact of ritual is hard to control. For the Rite of Penitence, four young people processed in with a large 'life-size' cross. Around the cross were hundreds of nails, hundreds of strips of bright red ribbon and a dozen large hammers. As we sang a lament, everyone was invited up to come and nail their sins to the cross. After two hundred people had come up, and after the 'music' of twelve hammers nailing ribbons to the cross, the cross was raised; Absolution was pronounced on the people in silence and then the cross was removed and replaced with a plain empty one. For some, the imagery of hammering a nail and red ribbon onto a cross to symbolize Jesus taking all our sins to the Cross was disturbing, for others it meant something quite different. Some wanted to linger at the cross, others wanted to get a drink and sing. Using ritual is messy. It illustrates that we are not all modernist constructs – 'Dolly the worshipper' – rather we are all very distinct individuals. What was certain was that no one was unmoved by the experience of participating in whatever way they wanted to or could handle. This was ritual which had made a connection.

One of the symptoms of our changing environment and culture is the changing attitude and understanding of truth. For many young people this has become 'whatever works for you'. Building a liturgy with different activities, movements, rituals, all culminating in the sharing of food and drink, meant that people could find their connections along the way in whatever way worked for them. We then gathered all this together in a common rite of communion.

THINKING IT THROUGH

Worshipping God is not done in just one way, as everyone has different tastes.

1. In what way are you listening to your young people?
2. How are you allowing them to share and speak?
3. What are the rites and rituals of your young people?
4. How do they express allegiance and community?
5. How can our existing rites and traditions speak into the lives of young people?
6. How can we let young people have the chance to express these in the life of the church?
7. How can we build community through rites and rituals both old and new?
8. What are the currencies of communication?
9. DO IT! Give young people permission to develop their own expression of worship. Support it and build the worship with them.

RITES AND RITUALS IN WORSHIP

SUMMARY

The theologian Walter Brueggemann believed one of the reasons for the Jewish exile to be their loss of confidence in using their temple vessels. In other words, they lost confidence in their rituals and practices. While I am sure it would be good to lose some of the stranger rituals in the Church altogether, there are a whole host of existing and as yet untapped rituals which need to be given fresh voice and to be reclothed to suit young people. As a Church we need to re-examine our use of rites and rituals and learn some more languages and incorporate them into the lifeblood of our worship. We also need to examine and use rites and rituals of young people today and see where connections between the Church and young people can be made. This is not the task of one part or tradition of the Church but for all of us as Christians who long to see young people come to a loving faith in Jesus Christ and taking their place within the Church and shaping it for the future. Using rites and rituals well helps young people become active participants in worship rather than passive observers, and can help young people to make a connection with their lives and with the reality of the living God, who in the rite and sacrament of Jesus gave his life that we and all people might live.

RITES AND RITUALS IN WORSHIP

Liturgies and outlines

Jonny Baker and Doug Gay, with Jenny Brown, *Alternative Worship*, SPCK, 2003.

Dot Gosling, Sue Mayfield, Tim Sledge and Tony Washington, *Youth Emmaus 2*, Church House Publishing, 2006.

Dan Kimball, *Emerging Worship: Creating worship gatherings for new generations*, Zondervan, 2004.

Mike Ridell, Mark Pearson and Cathy Kirkpatrick, *The Prodigal Project*, SPCK, 2004.

Sue Wallace, *Multi-Sensory Prayer*, Scripture Union, 2000.

Pete Ward (ed.), *The Rite Stuff*, Bible Reading Fellowship, 2004.

Pete Ward (ed.), *Mass Culture: The eucharist in the postmodern world*, SPCK, 1999.

www.textweek.com – a Roman Catholic site giving a variety of texts, sermons, liturgies and visuals from around the world; look out for 'Laughing Bird' from Australia.

www.cofe.anglican.org/worship/liturgy – all the Anglican authorized liturgies.

More general information about alternative worship on www.alternativeworship.org

Music

www.cjmmusic.co.uk – a variety of liturgies and music resources for the Eucharist. *Laudate* (modern music for the liturgy), available from www.decanimusic.co.uk *Complete Anglican Hymns Old and New*, Kevin Mayhew Ltd, 2001.

Visuals

www.google.co.uk and follow the links to images.

www.osbd.org – One Small Barking Dog – downloadable and DVD and video images for worship and meditation.

Just Worship 1& 2 – images for worship and more resources from www.ampublishing.net

5 CREATIVE APPROACHES TO EXISTING LITURGY

Jean Kerr

INTRODUCTION

Slumped in the back row sits the son of the churchwarden, the daughters of the PCC secretary and your own teenagers. While you're glad they are present there is no evidence that engagement with the service is actually taking place. Such scenes are taking place up and down the land in churches small and large.

This is not the place to debate the meaning of the word 'liturgy'. Let us for the sake of brevity follow the thinking in Mark Earey's excellent book *Liturgical Worship* (see 'Taking it further' below), where he states that

> liturgy is bigger than words; it encompasses what we do in the service as well as what we say. To use technical language, liturgy is 'rite': a pattern of words and actions that have meaning for a community. It includes silence, movement, posture, symbol. It engages us as whole persons: body, mind and spirit.[1]

To his definition I would urge us to add the physical setting of this rite, thus paying special attention to creating where possible an environment that is conducive to the making of 'sacred space'. Perhaps our problem is that the contents of the 'rite' no longer carry appropriate meaning for our young people.

THE ISSUE

Worship can feel like an endless stream of repetitive words that are the same week in, week out, be they spoken or sung. We need to hear the voices of the young people themselves:

> What I want is worship that is fresh every week with just enough of the familiar to keep me safe but with space to think my own thoughts with God. I need space to 'be' and music that is of my generation. *C. aged 17.*

> The space is great because the building is so high, but why do you spoil it with words? *M. aged 19, on cathedral worship.*

Is it simply a case of familiarity breeding contempt, or is there also within our young people a need to marry the ancient spiritual disciplines with a fresh symbolism and engagement? One might ask what are appropriate symbols and actions for the culture that our young people engage with. 'Liturgy' should be a box of tools that we use as connectors, enabling communication between God and his people; liturgy therefore should be seen as exciting and done in a way that enables this connection to happen.

'"Liturgy" should be a box of tools that we use as connectors, enabling communication between God and his people; liturgy therefore should be seen as exciting and done in a way that enables this connection to happen.'

So how do we deal with this problem of making liturgy appealing to young people without alienating the rest of the congregation or perhaps those in the congregation who dislike any kind of change? Should we also consider the issue of how we keep true to the tradition and distinctiveness of our particular church? A case of past meets (post)modern! I would want to contend that liturgy is only real and relevant when it grows from its historical roots, which support and aid current and future liturgical life.

THEORY AND BACKGROUND

A story is told of an American youth worker who was told by the vicar to 'do something' about making sure the young people stayed involved in worship. The youth worker talked with the young people and heard their call for more physical action in worship, a greater use of images and space and most of all a cry for a sense of the 'otherness' of God. So together they constructed a worship event that used some of the format of Taizé interwoven with interactive responses to prayer and challenges set in a worldwide context. The young people loved it and in time it drew large numbers to what was a sacred space for them. The vicar was delighted with its reported progress and was pleased to see that young people were also growing in small groups for Bible study. One or two even started to ask about vocations. Seeing this was such a good thing the vicar invited the youth group to lead a normal Sunday service. Again, people found its style engaging and enabling. A success? After the service, the story goes, the vicar meets with the youth worker and simply says, 'That was not an Episcopalian service.' So the issue of holding 'shape' versus 'fluidity' is the task of the ordinary church.

One young person has said:

> the liturgy can feel like an old person's mantra, a fast toneless spiel with exclusivity; without the service book it can leave you feeling lost and alone. Very rarely is there time to pause or reflect on what you are saying or what has been said.

Can the familiar texts and rituals exude new life?

The premise of this chapter is that while the worship event should have variety of content, style and pace, it should also have a consistency of theme running through it and a clear structure. Thus the chances for engagement are reinforced. It is our job to see the young people of the Church growing in faith and understanding. The liturgy of today may be steeped in tradition but that does not mean it is irrelevant or that it needs to be seen as 'boring'. The Creed is one example of this. Although this might be reeled off by many, the words said are life changing if the young people know what they are saying and why. To make a declaration of faith in this way is a big thing, especially if you know the full meanings of the words you are saying.

Therefore it is paramount that people really know deep down what the liturgy is all about. What do the words, actions, colours and silences really mean and what effect should they have on my life as I engage with them? Is saying or singing the words the only way of interacting with God and each other through worship?

It is also important to realize why we have liturgy and what significance it has to our faith and beliefs. If young people understand why we have liturgy and what the different parts mean, then they will begin to own the worship.

'It is also important to realize why we have liturgy and what significance it has to our faith and beliefs. If young people understand why we have liturgy and what the different parts mean, then they will begin to own the worship.'

It is quite an eye-opener to celebrate the Eucharist as if it were being played on a screen in front of us with a commentator at the side who is able to pause and freeze frame while giving a brief explanation. Perhaps more than just the young people would benefit!

NEED TO KNOW: Some solutions

This section will give you some ideas and suggestions on how we can use liturgy creatively in an everyday service without alienating the entire congregation. The ideas can be changed and adapted to be used as is suitable for each individual service. I have never yet found a book that gave me ideas which were just right for my congregation, but they did give me the chance to start thinking outside the box for myself – and God did the rest! All the examples below are used regularly with existing liturgy.

CASE STUDY 1: Liturgy as journey

First, an example of an interactive service of the Word that helped the whole congregation get in touch with liturgy as a journey. The size of the congregation was 120, of mixed ages. The 'rite' involved the congregation using different spatial zones.

The service was designed to try to enable each person to reach out to respond personally to God and do this by using a variety of different learning styles. The church building was separated into several zones including some in the hall. The start of the service followed a normal pattern of call to worship, hymn and opening reading. Direct instructions were given so everyone knew what to do as they were invited to bring something of their journey of exploration back at the end as the worshipping community gathered together. Parents of very tiny children were invited to work in the zones with their children. There was a creative area containing fabrics of varying textures, paint, drawing materials and recyclable materials for people to draw or make something with in response to their understanding of God. There was a noisy area containing instruments, especially percussion, to create a musical response. People were also invited to write a psalm in praise of God. There was a quiet reflective area with just a solitary candle and headlines from the newspaper, for people to quietly think and pray. A visual area contained various pictures of Christ displayed on a loop. There was also a food area allowing people the chance to marvel at God's provision.

This gave every person a chance to respond to God in a unique individual way. It also gave people time out to think carefully about what God really meant to them individually. It also reached out to different learning styles and personality types. At the end of the zone time, people gathered and the vicar led prayers offering the work done in the zones to God and the congregation joined together in a prayer of thanksgiving. The service ended with the hymn 'Great is thy faithfulness'.

This service worked because it contained only one element that was new – the use of 'zones'. The familiar gave safety to the new expression and held together the tension that always exists between the needs of individual and corporate worship. It was interesting that in the coffee time after the service old and young together shared their responses to the activity quite spontaneously.

Applying it to your local setting

This format is reliant on people taking part. However, it is possible to start on a small scale simply by having one responsive action that the congregation can take part in, and making sure that the leader of the service delivers that action first. Giving people permission to respond is really important. It is interesting to note that nowadays people seem more easily to engage in acts of respect and remembrance, e.g. the placing of flowers where someone has died, the signing of books of remembrance. Why not build this into liturgy?

No space to move around? Then simply follow the pattern and introduce zones by introducing pictures or symbols from the front for people to engage with. Why not take one aspect a week instead of the intercessions?

Setting and ambience

What about the setting for the service? Young people are very space aware, and ambience matters. Why not start the service with a simple home-written liturgy that enables the table to be set by members of the congregation – each article being placed on the table by someone of a different age, who might wish to give their own explanation of its importance. Thus we create sacred space within the normal building. Consider, if possible, using banners, flowers and/or artefacts to set the worship space with the theme of the day. Don't be afraid to use modern images, brand names, newspaper headlines. More importantly, ask young people to design the space themselves and introduce it as an aid to worship to the congregation, thus drawing people into worship whatever written words are used.

Light and liturgy

The simple act of having lots of nightlights in place and low music playing starts to say that here something of the God of mystery is happening. Don't be afraid to use Gregorian chant, or Taizé or classical music as a background.

> It was All Saints and we lit candles and placed them on a tinfoil cross. The effect was to help me understand that the reflection from my small amount of faith when placed with others is huge. The atmosphere in the church changed and we all picked up the holy hush. No one interfered to explain all this to us.
> *R. aged 14.*

Welcome as liturgy

Why not consider how people are welcomed into the service, again picking up the theme of the day. The style and nature of welcome can be hugely creative.

> It was Good Friday and I went under protest for the three hours' service. We were greeted at the door as individuals, welcomed and invited to allow someone to wash our hands to rid ourselves of all that would stop us worshipping God. I found it really strange but behind me I heard an old lady say that it was the first time for years that anyone had asked to touch her. I found that affected the journey to the cross for me. *A. aged 15.*

'It was Good Friday and I went under protest for the three hours' service. We were greeted at the door as individuals, welcomed and invited to allow someone to wash our hands to rid ourselves of all that would stop us worshipping God. I found it really strange but behind me I heard an old lady say that it was the first time for years that anyone had asked to touch her. I found that affected the journey to the cross for me.' A. aged 15.

The story is told

It is important that the language used during a service is accessible to all. Sometimes the words used can be old-fashioned and not understood by all. There are many different modern interpretations of the Bible available which can be used to help young people fully understand the passage: for example, *The Message Bible* and *The Street Bible*. Using an alternative translation can be the key to young people really understanding the word of God.

When leading any service it is always useful to try to vary the style and presentation to avoid any blasé attitudes or rote speaking. This can be as simple as having a dramatic reading. This can be in the form of several people reading different sections of the passage. Perhaps even more effective is when appropriate parts of the Bible are told as story. Whatever the age of the storyteller they can bring an insight into the passage.

> It was Mothering Sunday and an older woman told the story of the man born blind. She described it as if it was her own son with all the normal things like counting fingers and toes. We felt her despair at his blindness and the years of suffering while the child begged to earn money. When healed by Jesus we saw a mother changed. I started to think how I would be as a mother and that God was interested in that as well. *J. aged 14*.

Holding prayers

Interactive prayers are another way of enabling young people to engage with liturgy. These can be as simple or as creative as your imagination can create. Sometimes it helps people to have something physical to hold on to or to do something with. One example is of Jelly Baby Prayers. Each member of the congregation is given four different coloured jelly babies and each colour represents a people group, for example:

Red/Pink	=	friends and family
Green	=	people around the world
Yellow	=	those who are sick
Orange	=	children/young people

During the prayer time, as the intercessor reads the prayers each person holds the relevant jelly baby. We reflect on the issues around for that particular people group. The feel of the jelly baby in our hands reminds us of the fragility of their life. This is just an aid to help people really focus on what is being prayed for.

Images

For those who have data projectors or an OHP flooding the front with words or images or even shapes starts to engage more of our senses. Church Mission Society has produced a very powerful resource pack that contains many different images of Christ that have been produced over the years from all corners of the world (see the 'Taking it further' section).

> We had a loop of images of Christ playing. Some of them made me sit up sharp. I found them too harsh and disturbing – Could he suffer like that? Then came the one of the laughing Jesus and I just started laughing too. I think that was the first time I really knew that Jesus was real like me. *G. aged 13*.

Simply use a few of these images as an introduction to confession.

Reel faith?

The sermon slot often holds the greatest gripe for young people. Why not engage in a series of short film clips on a theme and simply pose, in question form, the issues that might arise for Christians? After all, giving space for people to sort out their response has a good precedent in Jesus' behaviour.

'The sermon slot often holds the greatest gripe for young people. Why not engage in a series of short film clips on a theme and simply pose, in question form, the issues that might arise for Christians? After all, giving space for people to sort out their response has a good precedent in Jesus' behaviour.'

Stories are always popular, so why not get old and young alike to share an experience and then simply gather them with biblical reflection? Choose a theme, such as ' "I am the bread of life" – what is it that really feeds us?' Being topical and relevant is essential. Young people will always appreciate topics in the national news and want to know what responses they can give to their non-Christian friends. Again, video clips of TV programmes and news items trigger responses. If you are really talented (and brave) why not discuss a sermon theme as a person really engaged with it – say a refugee being sent back or a woman trying to eke out a meal for a family in Zimbabwe. Issues of justice ring loud bells of relevance.

> After the service on refugees we could sit down with the preacher and fire questions at them. So much I thought I knew and so much I needed to challenge. It was all taken in good heart. I am still thinking it through. *H. aged 15.*

THINKING IT THROUGH

1. In what ways can you make your liturgy engaging for young people?
2. How can you weave in explanations of what the liturgy means in your services?
3. What opportunities do you have in your church to creatively approach liturgy?

CREATIVE APPROACHES TO EXISTING LITURGY

SUMMARY

Liturgy doesn't have to be the endless stream of words that sometimes meets us in church. Being creative with the liturgy can have a real impact on the church members and not just the young people. As highlighted in this chapter, being creative doesn't need to be difficult, and the effect that it can have on how young people engage in worship can be amazing. Using real-life examples and feedback from young people, this chapter has shown the importance of the worship setting and how little changes to the way we use the liturgy can have big effects.

CREATIVE APPROACHES TO EXISTING LITURGY

TAKING IT FURTHER

Useful web sites

www.artschaplaincy.org.uk
www.kevinfbates.com/reflections/creativepowerliturgy.htm
www.livingliturgy.com
www.iona.org.uk/wgrg/
www.grovebooks.co.uk/http:jonnybaker.blogs.com/jonnybaker/
http:jonnybaker.blogs.com/jonnybaker/worship_tricks/wt3.html
www.smallfire.org/intropage2.html
www.freshexpressions.org.uk

Useful books

Mark Earey, *Liturgical Worship*, Church House Publishing, 2002.
Richard Giles, *Creating Uncommon Worship*, Canterbury Press, 2004.

Group for Evangelization, *Equipping Your Church in a Spiritual Age*, Church House Publishing, 2005.

Rob Lacey, *The Street Bible*, Zondervan, 2003.

Michael Moynagh, *emergingchurch.intro*, Monarch, 2005.

Eugene Peterson, *The Message Bible*, Nav Press, 1993.

Wild Goose Worship Group, *Cloth for the Cradle*, Wild Goose Publications, 1997. Useful for Christmas.

Wild Goose Worship Group, *Stages on the Way*, Wild Goose Publications, 1998. Useful for Easter.

Music

Jumping in the House of God by World Wide Message Tribe (WEA).

trip. dancing about architecture by tripindicular tunes, www.tripwamsley.com/cd1.htm

The Mission by Ennio Morricone (Virgin).

Classical Ambience – the ultimate in calming classics (Music Club).

Echoes – The Einaudi Collection (BMG).

Resources

The Christ We Share, CMS, www.cms-uk.org

A-cross the World, CMS, www.cms-uk.org

Images for Worship, OSBD, www.osbd.org/

6 YOUNG PEOPLE AND ALL-AGE WORSHIP

Susie Mapledoram

INTRODUCTION

This chapter considers the tricky problem of young people's involvement in all-age worship. While many older members of the church may consider that all-age worship is something just for the younger age group, young people themselves often feel excluded from and patronized by it. This chapter suggests some ways of improving the situation.

THE ISSUE: The problem with all-age worship

Back in the book of the Acts of the Apostles we are introduced to the idea and purpose of Church. Hundreds of years later we are still striving to create a place for people to come together, to meet with each other and with God in worship, and to be resourced to go out and reach others. Many have seen the Church as a family and have made great efforts to make it accessible and participatory for children and young people.

This has led to the creation of special services, which the Church has called 'family worship' or 'all-age worship', the names signalling the clear intention that these are services in which the whole church is present (although there may be a crèche for the very smallest) and in which everyone can participate fully. However this isn't always the case . . .

It's Sunday morning, more than likely the last Sunday of the month. The uniformed groups are outside, shivering in the cold and as people walk into church they suddenly remember – its all-age worship today. It's not like the regular service where you have to meet the height restrictions like a ride at Thorpe Park. Many people with whom I have discussed all-age worship seem to have a sense of doom and foreboding about the whole idea of going to an all-age service. Before it has even started there is more a sense that this is something of an endurance test than a service to worship God.

The faces of many of the young people give away their reaction to the impending service and on some occasions a couple of them have taken great advantage of the busyness around the back of the church and made an early exit. Many of the young people I have talked to about all-age worship have the same feelings as the adults – 'It's not for us.' The perception is that it is geared for the children, and the adults 'have a laugh', but the young people find that it's all too patronizing for us'.

'Many of the young people I have talked to about all-age worship have the same feelings as the adults – "It's not for us."'

THEORY AND BACKGROUND

Let's look at some of the background and theory you need to know in working with young people and all-age worship.

A short history of all-age worship

All-age worship appeared in churches around the 1970s. The period following the Second World War saw an increase in the numbers of children born, but at the same time Sunday school numbers were declining. The Church saw the need to engage with families and provide something for the whole family unit and began to experiment with new kinds of service.

In much that I have read on all-age worship there seems to be little reflection on young people (11 to 18) and their response to this type of service. It is this group of people that I would like to concentrate on in this chapter. Are all-age services something that they enjoy, something that they want to be at and something that they can play a part in?

The biblical rationale

The Bible clearly states that the roles of those in the Body of Christ are all as valuable as each other:

> The eye cannot say to the hand, 'I have no need of you', nor again the head to the feet, 'I have no need of you.' On the contrary, the members of the body that seem to be weaker are indispensable.
>
> 1 Corinthians 12.21,22a

We have a responsibility to work out these biblical truths in how we do church and to see the value of the contributions of everyone. This can be a very positive opportunity to recognize and use the gifts of each person.

Young people and all-age worship

In my experience there have been times when churches have seen the young people as the awkward age group to cater for, to 'keep happy', and this has in some situations made the criteria for preparing the service more like a tick list of satisfying different age groups than a worshipful service that engages all ages. If our perspective is that of seeing young people as 'indispensable' surely that will not only change our approach to planning all-age worship but will also acknowledge the valuable contribution that young people can make to these services. It is important to see and acknowledge young people as a vital part of the body.

'If our perspective is that of seeing young people as "indispensable" surely that will not only change our approach to planning all-age worship but will also acknowledge the valuable contribution that young people can make to these services.'

Giving young people opportunities speaks powerfully about how we value them and respect their perspective on the world and how that affects their faith. Do we concentrate so much on keeping the children and the adults 'catered for' that we don't take on board the significant contribution that our young people can make to these services?

One of the key areas of the Church of England's National Youth Strategy *Good News for Young People* is Young People and Worship. The report speaks very positively about the development of the 'markedly different' patterns of worship that young people have been involved in and argues that these patterns should not been seen as 'experimental' or 'alternative', but as valid as other forms of worship and 'fully part of the worshipping community of the Church'.[1] This serves to reinforce the opinion and experience of many youth leaders, youth workers and ministers that young people have a significant contribution to make to the worshipping community of the Church. It goes beyond the once-in-a-while youth service, which is often interpreted as a service by youth for youth and usually ends with a patronizing round of applause for the 'youngsters' – it's about young people taking a key role in leading the whole congregation in worship. It's not about 'allowing' or 'letting them' take part – it's about giving young people a clean sheet and leaving them to it.

Many young people with whom I've worked have a very clear understanding of the importance of worship in their lives and what it means to them. This understanding has come about through growing up in a Christian family, being involved in a church, the teaching they have received in youth groups and going to larger events that have explored what worship is and why we do it. The general understanding is that worship is something that we do as a response to God and the gospel message. It something that is participatory and quite clearly is not something that is performed or seen as entertainment.

With these thoughts in mind, are we too quick to produce something *for* young people which is *performed* to *entertain* them in church or are we actively seeking to engage with young people by involving them and creating a worship where they feel that they can participate. Are we treating young people more like consumers than participators?

'Are we too quick to produce something *for* young people which is *performed* to *entertain* them in church or are we actively seeking to engage with young people by involving them and creating a worship where they feel that they can participate. Are we treating young people more like consumers than participators?'

Our response

Young people's response to worship in church generally is 'whatever', and the consistent response to all-age services and other times when the young people are in the services is that what is aimed at them is often quite patronizing and tokenistic. The 1996 *Youth A Part* report states that:

> This caricature of worship for young people is held by many well-meaning people. Using a guitar in the service often represents a huge stride by the congregation to welcome young people into a service. However, for the young people it may not be enough, and can be seen as a rather patronizing gesture.[2]

Whether we admit that this is an issue within our own congregation or not, the evidence will be seen in the response from young people to all-age worship services. What we do with that response is essentially how we make all-age worship something that does work and genuinely reaches all ages within the church. It means taking the risky step of asking questions like 'Are you enjoying all-age worship at this church?' or 'How could we make the all-age services more relevant to you as young people?' We may well know some of the answers to these questions already but by valuing the thoughts and feelings of the young people, a worthwhile new dialogue could begin and cooperation between the leadership of your church and the young people. An idea expressed by a young person could be the focus for your next service and wouldn't it make sense for those who have suggested it to do it?

Good News for Young People states that worship that is youth-led is not alternative or experimental but that we should 'learn from the experience of the pioneers'.[3] Surely this could be easily translated into our all-age worship?

CASE STUDIES: Doing all-age worship better

The issue that we are addressing here is the very question of whether young people are enjoying, experiencing and engaging with all-age worship and we are looking at ways of valuing and encouraging their contribution and participation. The following examples illustrate ways of doing this well.

I was involved in the youth work of a church that used to have between five or six all-age services a year. These took place for a variety of reasons, for example to give the children's and youth leaders a break on a Sunday morning so that they could attend an all-age service with their friends and/or family. There would be a variety of responses from the young people at the prospect of an all-age service, ranging from 'this will be dire' to 'this will be entertaining'. But they would be there. It would, essentially, be a service focused on children and young people, with a short sermon, plenty of action songs and confectionery would usually make an appearance somewhere!

There was an opportunity to coordinate an all-age service and it was at this stage that I thought about how the young people could engage with this. I met with the young people and we discussed the different elements of the service and how the young people would run things. I didn't say, 'You do this and you do that.' The theme was flat on the table and the young people made it three-dimensional. A number of the young people joined with some adults from the congregation to create a worship group for the service. This was nothing unusual as the regular worship group consisted of young people and adults, but it gave the young people an opportunity to organize the songs and lead the worship. All the elements of the service were planned and carried out by the young people, apart from the sermon (which *they* decided I would do!), but they sought to involve children and adults in various parts. The young people wanted to catch the attention and participation of the children by getting people to write prayers on Post-its, sticking them to helium balloons and releasing them. The response from the congregation was very positive, many commenting that 'this is what church should be like all the time'. The response from the young people was the same, and for them the whole experience of putting the service together and their participation had been very positive. It should be said that this whole experience came on the back of some teaching around worship and talking around the whole issue of worship not being entertainment but our response to God.

On another occasion I took a group of young people to a Rock Mass. I had heard about it from some friends and some of the young people in my youth group were keen to go. I had no idea what to expect, but one thing I did know about this service was that young people played a big part in it. It was a Rock Mass by definition – a Communion service with Queen songs in between a few Wesley hymns. It did appear that it was very much an adult-directed service with young people filling in the gaps. They would lead from up front but from conversations afterwards it became apparent that they did what the adults suggested. But it appeared that everyone involved was happy with that set-up. The young people and adults had a good working relationship and the young people were happy with their level of involvement.

NEED TO KNOW: Some basic principles for better all-age worship

A colleague of mine in the Diocese of Blackburn recently wrote a dissertation on all-age worship and as part of this piece of work he made some very practical suggestions for basic principles for these services, some of which are listed here:

- Do not be patronizing.
- Do include, do not exclude.
- Keep the service shorter.
- Plan with a team – a group of people will bring so much more to a service. This situation gives people the chance to take responsibility for areas of a service where they feel their gifts lie.
- Keep the talk short.
- Value silence.
- Encourage relationships – the value of working with different people from different age groups can be a great opportunity to build relationships.
- Use visuals and use stories.
- Be interactive.
- Use movement.
- Be genuine.
- Think about your environment – where the service is being held.[4]

THINKING IT THROUGH

1. In your church context, how do you engage young people in all-age worship?
2. How can you develop the youth work in your church by involving young people in organizing all-age worship?
3. What are your reflections on all-age worship in your church?
4. What is the ethos behind all-age worship in your church setting?

5. In what way can you encourage the development of gifts and skills amongst your young people?
6. As we seek to build up the confidence of young people, how can we do the same with other members of our congregation?
7. Are there ways of sharing good practice in all-age services with other churches?
8. If involving young people in the organization and participation of all-age worship has such positive outcomes, in what other areas of church life could young people be involved where they are not involved at present?

YOUNG PEOPLE AND ALL-AGE WORSHIP

SUMMARY

The question of whether all-age worship really works in relation to young people is a contextual one. Each church is unique, with its own distinctive congregation, style of leadership and approach to worship, so in each case the answer to the question will be different. How we do all-age worship in our own setting will be dependent on local factors. However, I'm convinced through experience and talking to young and old alike, that our approach should come from a participatory perspective rather than seeing it as an opportunity to entertain the younger members of our congregation.

YOUNG PEOPLE AND ALL-AGE WORSHIP

The conveyer belt of resources is constantly bringing along really good material to use with young people, which can easily be adapted to church services. As with all resources, you can pick and mix the content and adjust it for your situation. However, there aren't a huge amount of resources around on all-age worship specifically for young people – 90% of resources for all-age worship contain activities for children with little consideration for young people.

Youthwork magazine has a resources section in each edition. This contains 'ready-to-use' meetings, ideas for drama, ways of using tracks from recent albums, clips from films, pictures in teaching and worship, and ideas for multi-sensory worship. These are easy to use and can be incorporated into a service as well as being used as a stand-alone resource.

The *Multi-Sensory* books give plenty of ideas on different ways of doing worship, prayers, Bible teaching and also includes a book on complete multi-sensory worship sessions. This style of worship is not everyone's cup of tea but they are worth a look to get some ideas to complement what you might already have planned.

Sue Wallace, *Multi-Sensory Prayer*, Scripture Union, 2000.
Sue Wallace, *Multi-Sensory Church*, Scripture Union, 2002.
Sue Wallace, *Multi-Sensory Scripture*, Scripture Union, 2005.

Use of film clips is increasingly popular in services, primarily to capture the attention of the children and young people, and to provide a visual for a teaching point in the talk/sermon. There is a series of books available called *Videos That Teach*, which give you the title of the film, where to find the specific clip and an explanation of a theme that the clip links into. For example, films such as *Monsters Inc*, *Toy Story* and other popular animated films can be used and have an appeal factor to both children and young people. OK . . . yes . . . and adults.

Eddie James and Doug Fields, *Videos That Teach 1, 2, 3* and *4*, Zondervan, 1999, 2002, 2004, 2006.

Using video clips from films that may well be in the DVD collections of your young people is a way of connecting with their culture and has the potential to create some good conversation after the service about the rest of the films in the series! Next thing you know you'll be sitting through all six *Star Wars* films in a weekend marathon, surviving on popcorn and Dr Pepper!

Having a bookshelf full of resource books, drama books and teaching books will no doubt give us ideas to work on for many services, but, of course, our most valuable and 'indispensable' resource is our young people.

Suggestions for further reading

A. Barton, *All-Age Worship,* Grove No. 126, 1993.

T. Stratford, *Interactive Preaching: Opening the word then listening*, Grove No 144, 1998.

Jim Trood, 'Is all-age worship possible in the Church of England in the 21st century?', MA thesis, St John's College, Nottingham, 2002.

www.familyworship.org.uk/howtowl2.htm – Practical pointers for all-age worship.

NEW FORMS OF WORSHIP

SECTION 3

In Section 3 we explore new ways of worshipping. I start by helping you think through ways that you can experiment with new forms of worship within the context of a regular service, as well as set up something different. Craig Abbott then looks at the role of youth congregations and youth churches and considers how these relate to the 'adult' church. Pete Maidment then looks at what we mean by and some examples of 'alternative worship'.

7 EXPERIMENTING WITH NEW FORMS OF WORSHIP

Mark Montgomery

INTRODUCTION

Experimenting with new forms of worship isn't as hard or as scary as it sounds! For some, just the words 'new forms' puts them off straight away. In this chapter I hope to help you explore ways that you can use new forms or different styles of worship in regular services as well as special services specifically designed to engage young people. I share with you some of the stories of good practice that I have seen working in churches, as well as giving you some practical ideas for engaging in worship with young people.

First, we should dispel the myth that experimenting with a new form of worship will take you away from your church's tradition and completely alienate the rest of the congregation. For the purposes of this chapter I am going to define a new form of worship as something which is different and new to your church family. I would also like to suggest that a new form of worship is something that can be happening in your church already, in home groups, Sunday school or even when the young people lead prayers every now and then.

'We should dispel the myth that experimenting with a new form of worship will take you away from your church's tradition and completely alienate the rest of the congregation.'

THE ISSUE: What is a new form of worship?

In my job as a diocesan youth officer in the Church of England I have many churches ask the question 'How can we make our worship more attractive to young people and young adults?' But they don't know where to start, or how to break into the normal format of their Sunday morning worship, often for fear of upsetting other members of the congregation.

When experimenting with new forms of worship there is no set pattern or format. For some, it will mean running a completely different type of service at a different time and possibly day to the regular Sunday services. Yet for others, it will be integrating into a regular service different activities or things they have seen work elsewhere. Some congregations will welcome both and some will welcome only the latter.

So what is a new form of worship? As stated earlier I define a new form of worship as something different to what you do already. And you are probably experimenting already without being aware of it! From the simple act of having interactive prayers or a sermon that uses pictures, to a whole new service aimed specifically at a certain group of people (probably young), experimenting can be simple or more in-depth, it's up to you. In this chapter we will focus on two areas of experimenting and explore the pitfalls and joys of each through case studies. One is a whole worship experience aimed at young people and the other is an example of integrating new ideas that might engage young people with a regular service.

'A new form of worship as something different to what you do already. And you are probably experimenting already without being aware of it!'

THEORY AND BACKGROUND

The first question we should address when opening up this topic is 'should we' make our services or worship more appealing to young people, or 'should they' learn to conform like their parents and their parents' parents did?

The world outside the Church has changed dramatically over the past 20 or even 10 years and young people now find themselves with a great deal more choice of activities and interests. In addition, young people are now listened to and even consulted on how their world is formed. With this in mind, churches need to address the role of young people within them.

As young people are just as much participants in the church as adults there should definitely be space for young people to be able to interact with the normal services provided by your church. I wouldn't necessarily say that we should be making our worship 'attractive' to young people but if we get the balance right, church worship should be accessible to all ages.

One of the most interesting things I see when I visit churches experimenting with new forms of worship for or by young people is that in many of the cases the service or activity aimed specifically at young people also attracts a wider congregation. In many cases, these services do become 'all-age'.

There are examples throughout history of people making worship experiences relevant to specific groups. Many of these have come out of a heart to work with particular groups of people: for example, John Wesley had a particular heart for working with the poor, so a new form of ministry and worship developed, which we know today as Methodism. In Chapter 9 Pete Maidment describes three other significant worship movements that have developed over recent years. All of these examples have helped the Christian Church move forward and grow in numbers.

One of the main examples of churches experimenting with new forms of worship and growing in number was the Early Church in Acts. One of the main reasons for this was that they were following a pattern set down for them by Jesus and the Old Testament. At the end of Acts 2, we read how the people who accepted the Apostles' teachings not only worshipped together at the Temple but also in their homes and when they met together (Acts 2.41–47). If we continue reading through Acts, we see many places and ways in which the Early Church came together to worship and praise God. Jackie Cray sums up her findings about children in the Early Church as follows:

- The children are present with the adults at the main worship events.
- The children are welcomed, received and attended to as participants.
- The children are the responsibility of the whole extended family (Old Testament) or church gathering (New Testament).[1]

She also comments: 'I'm convinced from my reading of the New Testament and my studies of early communities of the Christian church that the upbringing and nurture of children was the responsibility of the whole household gathering.'[2]

This was an all-age church with people of every age meeting together and living in community.

If you think of your church, you may have activities aimed at all ages, from groups for mums and tots, children and young people and the elderly to home groups. These are aimed at involving the whole church congregation, but often issues arise when bringing these groups together in a corporate act of worship. It takes a lot of time and effort to create a space where all ages are engaged and participating. At this point, some churches decide it is easier to have to have separate acts of worship for particular groups, but this can mean other sectors of the congregation becoming alienated. I hear many times from churches that whenever they run a family service half of the congregation doesn't turn up, as the service is really aimed at children (a more in-depth analysis of this issue can be found in Chapter 6). This is a generalization but is a common situation across the country. We should, however, be thinking of the Early Church as an example of all-age church, where people of all ages came together to praise and worship. When it comes to experimenting with new forms of worship you need the congregation to be open to new ways of worshipping, especially if you are looking to incorporate ideas into the main service. This might be done through a process of teaching leading up to the changes. Some examples could be a series of talks exploring how people learn and how that helps them meet with God, or a series using biblical examples of different ways of worshipping. It is also important even if you are setting up a separate worship experience to have the whole congregation with you. You might want to have open church meetings explaining the changes to services. This will allow people to comment on the

'Some churches decide it is easier to have to have separate acts of worship for particular groups, but this can mean other sectors of the congregation becoming alienated.'

changes but also hear the full story behind them. I have seen this model work particularly well when churches have explored the idea of admitting children to communion before confirmation. This helps everyone understand where the worship experience fits into the wider context of regular church activities. Having the whole church on board with the experiment helps the people running the experiment not to feel separate from the church and allows the whole church to own it.

NEED TO KNOW: Where do you start?

So where do we start when experimenting with new forms of worship? I highlighted earlier that I am going to look at two ways of experimenting: using new ideas in a regular act of worship, and the other, starting a whole new experience. Both these activities have been used to encourage young people to become part of the regular worshipping community both as participants and leaders. To help us reflect on the two ways of experimenting I will be using case studies to help us think through the issues, as well as raising some questions to think about.

Using new ideas in regular worship

This is one way of experimenting that has become very easy in churches today. It has become very acceptable in many churches to have activities like dramatized Bible readings, sketches, illustrative sermons and interactive prayers in regular worship times. But for those churches where this hasn't happened, this can be seen as experimenting with a new form of worship. It might be normal to have some of these activities in, say, a family service but not in other monthly services for a fear that it might upset people. So how do we go about starting to integrate some of the activities above which can engage young people in the service?

CASE STUDY 1: A youth group leads a Remembrance Day service

It was Remembrance Sunday and the youth group had been asked to lead the 6 p.m. evening service. The youth group in the church met on a Thursday night and while some of the members attended church regularly or occasionally, others didn't at all – a common youth group situation. The vicar and one of the youth group leaders had mooted the idea of young people leading the service to both the worship committee and the youth group and both had agreed. For many of the evening congregation, Remembrance Sunday was an important part of their year, as many had either lived through part of the war or grew up in post-war times. The young people wanted to be sensitive to the issue but also use new ideas to help everyone attending engage with the idea of remembrance. The vicar also thought it was important not to stray too far from the familiarity of the normal service structure.

'For many of the evening congregation Remembrance Sunday was an important part of their year, as many had either lived through part of the war or grew up in post-war times. The young people wanted to be sensitive to the issue but also use new ideas to help everyone attending engage with the idea of remembrance.'

After a little research on the web one of the leaders found an outline of a service on www.altworship.org.uk created by the alt.worship collective in Bradford. The youth group decided to take parts of that service and integrate them into the worship. So within the normal structure of hymns, prayers and sermon the young people added in at least two of the ideas from the alt.worship web site.

The first asked members of the congregation to rip out stories in newspapers relating to conflict and violence and pin them to a board. Added to this, the congregation were asked to write prayers on paper outlines of poppies, and also asked to light a candle in prayer and add that to the foot of the cross. After these activities the young people sprinkled poppy petals down the aisle to link these activities as one whole act of remembrance.

Reflection

The ideas in the above case study were simple, non-threatening to the wider congregation and helped the young people engage with the subject through their active participation. Young people currently live in a visual and interactive world where they participate and engage with activities through seeing and doing. A lot of the time church isn't participatory or visual within acts of worship.

The idea of asking members to light a candle as part of prayer has been around for centuries. How many times do you ask the congregation to do it during the Sunday service? Asking people to use a newspaper to make visual representations about a subject, or during prayers, is simple and easy. Asking the congregation to move around the church during a service might, at first, feel a little threatening, as this is not necessarily the norm, but is a simple way of encouraging people to interact with the subject.

These simple ideas can be interwoven into any service and for some might be massive steps away from what they are used to. However, they are ways of experimenting with a new form of worship in an easy and non-threatening way.

Starting a new worship experience

This can be seen as one of the easiest ways of experimenting with a new form of worship as it might not have a massive impact on the rest of the congregation. The new worship experience might take place on a different day or at a different time to a regular congregation, or even take the place of a regular service. Whichever way is chosen, people can choose not to attend.

CASE STUDY 2: Creating a new service

The church was the only Anglican church in a growing market town. Because of this unique situation the church was rather large (in size and congregation) and was starting to attract people who had moved into the town from various Anglican traditions. Many of the church wanted to create a worship experience that would reflect some of the new worship activities and experiences that were happening around the country and also to attract members of the youth group to regularly attend a worship service. It was clear that they didn't want to create a 'youth service', but something that would be informal, non-threatening and engaging for all ages. The make-up of the planning group comprised a broad cross-section of church membership, and included clergy and youth leaders as well as other adults, although no young people were asked to be involved at the outset.

It was agreed that the worship experience shouldn't be of any one particular style but subjects would be picked and then the leader/preacher would be able to respond to the subject and lead activities to help people engage with that subject. As this was a team project each member would be utilized across the cycle of services using their particular skills. This meant that each service took a different form, including Taizé-style services, the use of images and films in preaching, interactive prayers and new worship music (the church normally uses organ music). It was also hoped that the service would take place at an accessible time for everyone and this was deemed to be a Sunday evening.

Reflection

This service has attracted a wide range of ages from the many service congregations that the church has. This has included some young people, but it has been most successful in drawing in young adults in their twenties and early thirties and older young people aged between sixteen and eighteen. One of the reasons why young people have not come in large numbers is thought to be because they were not involved in the service planning, but their participation is being developed over time.

In each case study the whole church warmly welcomed and praised the service. The first as it helped people look at the subject in a different way and also blazed a trail for some of the ideas to be used by all the church congregations and not just in the evening service. There was some resistance to some of the ideas being used in the morning service at first but that was overcome by helping some of the congregation to understand that the church is for everyone.

'There was some resistance to some of the ideas being used in the morning service at first but that was overcome by helping some of the congregation to understand that the church is for everyone.'

The second case study is a living and worshipping service that can be found in a church in South Cheshire twice a month. The main issue faced was to stop it being seen as a completely separate activity and not as one of the regular Sunday services. However, the diversity of people attracted to the service has helped this. It has become one of the few services in the church that attracts members from most, if not all, of the church's activity groups, including the young people.

THINKING IT THROUGH

1. What new forms of worship does your church already experiment with?
2. Do you think we should be making our church services relevant to young people or should they just conform?
3. Which of the two case studies relates most to your church?
4. How would either of the services go down in your church?
5. Which of the two examples would fit in your church and how would you go about implementing it?

EXPERIMENTING WITH NEW FORMS OF WORSHIP

SUMMARY

In this chapter I have tried to highlight some of the issues that arise from experimenting with new forms of worship, and some practical ideas of how to start experimenting in your church. I hope that you will see that experimenting can be as simple and easy as lighting candles, or can be something very different, new and exciting. My hope is that you will start experimenting in your church and help everyone engage in worship, especially young people.

EXPERIMENTING WITH NEW FORMS OF WORSHIP

Web sites

www.altworship.org.uk – have a look through the resources and links.

http://jonnybaker.blogs.com/jonnybaker/worship_tricks

www.freshexpressions.org.uk

Books

R. Bolger and E. Gibbs, *Emerging Churches: Creating Christian communities in postmodern cultures*, SPCK, 2006.

D. Kimball, *The Emerging Church: Vintage Christianity for new generations*, Zondervan, 2003.

D. Kimball, *Emerging Worship: Creating worship gatherings for new generations*, Zondervan, 2004.

L. Sweet (ed.), *The Church in Emerging Culture: Five perspectives*, Zondervan, 2003.

Pete Ward, *Selling Worship*, Authentic Media Publishing, 2005.

Practical resources to use with young people on worship and prayer

S. Case, *The Book of Uncommon Prayer: Contemplative and celebratory prayers and worship services for youth ministry*, Zondervan, 2002.

DIY Worship, CPAS (Pathfinder Series).

DIY Celebrations, CPAS (Pathfinder Series).

Prayer Zone, CPAS (Pathfinder Series).

The other chapters in this section list further resources and ideas to help you take issues raised in this chapter further.

8 WHAT'S THE LINK BETWEEN 'YOUTH CHURCH' AND 'ADULT CHURCH'?

Craig Abbott

INTRODUCTION

The aim of this chapter is to explore some of the issues around the growing number of youth churches and youth congregations in England. By 'youth churches' I am referring to churches established for a single generation with no direct links in terms of authority and accountability to another church. In talking about 'youth congregations' I refer to worshipping communities of predominantly young people which have a connection to an established church, taking the form of, for instance, shared leadership and decision making, accountability, shared buildings and so on.

THE ISSUE

The question has been asked what, if any, is the link between these relatively new expressions of church, be they 'churches' or 'congregations', and the traditional churches and traditional congregations. Indeed, the question could be asked 'Do there need to be links between the different churches and congregations?' If so, are there effective ways in which they can be linked or do we just accept that in an increasingly fragmented world the Church needs to offer an increasingly varied menu of expressions of church to meet the needs of a diverse culture?

In this chapter I will unpack some of these issues and questions. We will look at some examples of existing youth churches and congregations and what their relationship is to the traditional church.

THEORY AND BACKGROUND

Before proceeding any further with this discussion it's important to establish loose definitions of some of the terms used in this chapter.

What is Church?

Here the term 'traditional church' will be used to refer to those local manifestations of church found in most communities, that is, the Church of England parish churches or equivalent in other denominations, the congregations of which would generally meet on Sunday. Both the church building itself and the structure and content of the coming together of the Body of Christ are considered traditional for the purposes of this chapter. In contrast, 'youth church' or 'youth congregation' is used here to mean a church or congregation established to meet the needs of a specific age group that meets apart from the traditional church. The building may well be a borrowed 'traditional' church building, but the style and time of meeting would reflect the culture of the young people that the church is trying to cater for.

Another major question posed by this chapter is 'What is meant by the term *church*?' Although there are vast tomes on this subject, a basic understanding would be helpful here. I have found the following five points useful in my understanding of church. I have taken these from the principles I see at work in the Early Church in the book of Acts.

1. Worshipping God

This is a fundamental principle of 'church'. As Pete Ward has suggested, 'The only adequate response to the gospel is to worship God.'[1] Worship is at the heart of the Christian community. Worship will be expressed in a variety of ways but it is one of the elements that sets the Church apart from secular communities. The main focus of a church isn't what its members have to offer each other but what they have to offer God, and their lives being transformed by encountering him in worship. Worship acknowledges that church isn't primarily about the needs of an individual or a community; although as we shall see these are both important principles of church; worship puts Christ at the centre of all that the Church stands for.

> **'The main focus of a church isn't what its members have to offer each other but what they have to offer God, and their lives being transformed by encountering him in worship.'**

2. Community of care

As well as having an emphasis on the centrality of Christ, the Church also has a duty of care to its members, to be a place where they are accepted, listened to and able to make a contribution. This principle of church life can be summed up in the passage from John 13.35: 'By this everyone will know that you are my disciples, if you have love for one another.'

3. 'Every member ministry' – all are involved

Taking on the principles outlined in 1 Corinthians 12 about understanding the church as a body, church is a place where every member has the opportunity to be involved in the 'body' life of the church. Indeed, the church community benefits from having all its members working together.

4. Outward looking – missionary

The Church has to have a mission-imperative. Mission is at the core of Church's existence. 'The Church is both the fruit of God's mission – those whom he has redeemed, and the agent of his mission-the community through whom he acts for the world's redemption.'[2]

For the Church, mission is about being involved in the ultimate mission of God to redeem the world. God is constantly at work in the world and it is the task of the Church to keep in step with his activity in the world. Mission isn't the Church's initiative, it is God's, but so often the Church has failed to take the initiative to keep up with God's activity in the world.

5. Growth and change – discipleship

By growth I don't necessarily mean numerical addition to the Church's numbers but the personal growth of the Church's members. Part of the Church's role is to be an agent of change, affecting its members through personal growth and effecting change in its community and the world.

Whatever your views, it's important to acknowledge that our personal view of church, our *ecclesiology*, greatly affects the way we do church and this is no less the case when talking about youth church. It may even be the case that your view of 'church' doesn't allow you to accept youth church as a valid expression of church.

Never the twain shall meet?

Christ desires unity; he prayed for it in the garden of Gethsemane before his arrest, trial and execution (John 17.23) and there are benefits of mixing age groups together. However, there are also benefits of having unique congregations and churches for specific age groups. I would argue that the two need not be mutually exclusive and there are ways in which they can be effectively linked for the benefit of both. Here we shall explore the arguments on both sides.

It has been the trend within the past 15 years for churches, youth workers and other agencies to provide alternative expressions of church specifically aimed at young people. Some of these were originally designed to provide a bridge between young people and mainstream church; others were established as distinctive youth churches in themselves, with no aim to connect to the wider Church. My intention isn't to say which, if any, is the best model, as different models will work differently depending on the context. I intend to highlight some of the issues involved and hopefully provide some reflections to encourage you to think through the issues for your particular situation.

'It has been the trend within the past 15 years for churches, youth workers and other agencies to provide alternative expressions of church specifically aimed at young people.'

CASE STUDY 1: Church Plant, Christ Church, Pennington

Church Plant at Christ Church, Pennington is a good example to look at. Entitled Church Plant to reflect the fact that it was a church planted in a cultural framework relevant to young people rather than a building planted in a specific geographical location, the initial aim was to establish a youth congregation that met at the same time as the 'adult' church but in a separate building with the overall aim of feeding the young people back into the 'adult' congregation after a period of time. However, the time of the meeting changed to make it more accessible to young people and the style and content reflected the culture of the young people involved and so the bridging strategy was unsuccessful. Those who attended the youth congregation or who came to faith through its witness, didn't make it to the adult church. However, looked at from another angle, the story is one of success. The initiative won young people to Christ and gave them a place to express and explore their faith and came to be viewed as being as valid an expression of church as any other.

Reflection

It seems clear that those young people who were involved in or who came to faith as a result of the work done by Church Plant were attracted to a gospel that was presented in a culturally relevant way. They were also able to worship and express their faith in God in ways that connected with their culture. The sponsoring church of Christ Church, Pennington wasn't an expression of church with which many of them could connect.

CAN YOUTH CONGREGATIONS AND CHURCHES BE JUSTIFIED?

As Bishop Graham Cray has expressed it:

> youth congregations are not a bridging strategy. They are not a temporary holding camp where young people can be acclimatized to existing church. It is not a bridge to the real thing. These groupings take responsibility for worship, pastoral care, mission and evangelism. To their members they are the only real thing they know. It is an experience of the Church of Jesus Christ.[3]

Here Bishop Graham justifies the existence of youth congregations as legitimate expressions of church in their own right without the young people needing to 'progress' on to adult expressions of church. It is worth noting that youth congregations, with their connection to an established traditional church, do still offer an opportunity for young people to be integrated into it, whereas those who establish separate and distinctive youth churches provide no such opportunity.

'Youth congregations, with their connection to an established traditional church, do still offer an opportunity for young people to be integrated into it, whereas those who establish separate and distinctive youth churches provide no such opportunity.'

There are ecclesiological issues raised by single-generation churches. Outlined in more detail in *Mission-shaped Church*, the Homogenous Unit Principle, as it has been phrased states: 'people like to become Christians without crossing racial/linguistic/class/cultural barriers'.[4]

This appears to be what was happening at Christ Church, Pennington – young people were coming to faith and expressing that faith within their own cultural context. Some have argued that this method of church is flawed because Jesus came to reconcile relationships not just between *God* and *humankind* but also between *person* and *person*, breaking down cultural barriers and thus negating the need for single-generation churches. In response, one could argue that cultural diversity is part of God's amazing and vast creation. We could also argue that because Jesus was born into a specific cultural context, that church too, can justify some expressions being planted in a specific cultural context.

However, single-generation churches may suffer as a result of their nature. They may not benefit from the wisdom and life experience of older generations. There may also have to be a process of reinventing the single-generation churches, particularly in regard to youth churches, as the congregation will naturally grow up and their culture will change. So, while single-generation churches pose some interesting ecclesiological issues it is clear that they can provide an expression of church for the culture they seek to reach. Multi-generation and multicultural churches may be the ideal situation for churches to aim for, but it seems to me that remaining true to the foundational principles of church is more important. Referring back to the five principles outlined above, these are potentially achievable in either a single-generation or multi-generation church context.

'While single-generation churches pose some interesting ecclesiological issues it is clear that they can provide an expression of church for the culture they seek to reach.'

Having said all this, youth churches and mainstream churches needn't be mutually exclusive. Even though youth congregations aren't necessarily the bridging strategy that some would hope for, there are ways in which the two can coexist in the same area and benefit from each other. A youth congregation that has some affinity with a traditional church can draw on that church's resources. There could be crossover of personnel, access to sacramental ministry, wider training and networking opportunities. It also provides the opportunity for a relationship of accountability to exist between the churches. The youth congregations have a great deal to teach the Church about their flexible attitude to church, and it is my belief that they will inform the nature of church in the future. So, while youth congregations can't be expected to exist to inflate the numbers in traditional church, the two needn't be totally separate and can coexist in a healthy relationship. A good example of this mutuality is the story of Eternity in Bracknell.

CASE STUDY 2: Eternity, Bracknell

The evolution of Eternity can be read in Encounters on the Edge No. 4, *Eternity – The Beginning*.[5] A group of friends in their twenties took over a youth service at their church which was originally planned by older adults. The service grew and young people came to faith through the work. In order to maintain the young people a network of small groups was formed. The work has grown and developed since its beginning but it has always maintained contact with the local church. Mark Meardon, who was instrumental in establishing Eternity, is quoted as saying:

> The most important thing is that keeping with our mother church is imperative. Being accountable is so necessary. We would not have gone ahead with planting Eternity if we did not have 100% blessing from St Michael's. The prayer support, teaching and care from them is invaluable.[6]

St Michael's, the 'mother church', is very supportive of Eternity and they have sought to have a good relationship with the deanery and the diocese with Mark being licensed. What Eternity demonstrates is that church provision for young people can have a healthy and interdependent relationship with a mother church.

NEED TO KNOW: How to start a youth congregation

If you feel that starting a youth congregation may be the right step in your mission to young people, some practical suggestions may be helpful. This section poses a lot of questions for you to ask about your context and situation as well as raising some practicalities to think about. They are in no particular order of importance.

Ensure it is born out of a felt need

One of the fundamental principles to consider when thinking about a youth congregation is to ensure that it is born out of a felt need rather than importing a strategy that has worked elsewhere. It's easy to fall in to the trap of setting something up because it works somewhere else and 'looks good'.

> It is tempting in our society of standardized parts, off-the-shelf everything and pre-packaged solutions, to look for ready-made models of church or worship that we can buy into. It seems to work in Iona, so let's do Celtic. Alpha seems to work in Kensington, so let's translate it into Swahili. They seem to be doing well in Willow Creek, let's give it a go in Burnt Oak. While cross-fertilization of ideas is to be encouraged, unless they are adapted to the local situation, they run the risk of failing to thrive.[7]

We need to ensure that the idea of establishing a youth congregation or church has developed from a real need in that particular church or community. And there needs to be clear understanding about how you define church. As I said earlier, your ideas about church will inform the way in which you 'do' church.

'We need to ensure that the idea of establishing a youth congregation or church has developed from a real need in that particular church or community. And there needs to be clear understanding about how you define church.'

Make a community profile

An invaluable exercise to undertake for any church is some sort of community profiling. Understanding the needs of your community can greatly affect the way in which you do church within your community. There are a variety of sources where information about your community can be obtained: try the local library, Connexions/local youth providers, local history centre, census information, local council offices – county and borough, Citizens Advice Bureau, local universities/FE colleges, schools and education authorities; try researching the geography, finding out about transport, talking to older people about the history of your community; talk to other churches that have been in the community for some time as they will have a good grasp of the needs of the area.

How are the young people involved?

It is also important to ask how young people are involved in the process. Has the idea come from them? What role do they have in the shaping of the congregation? What role will they have in the implementing and running of the project?

What will your relationship be with the traditional church?

Will there be any connection with the traditional church? As we saw earlier, this allows for healthy, accountable relationships to develop between your leadership and more experienced leaders. Links to a mainstream church will also provide access to opportunities for training and networking. Where a youth congregation is established as an extended part of the ministry of a parish church, as in the example from Eternity in Bracknell, the connections should be easier to establish and maintain providing that the leadership of the church is supportive. However, problems may arise where a youth congregation stretches over one or more parish boundaries. There are guidelines that will inform a project in this situation. The report *A Measure for Measures: In Mission and Ministry: Report of the Review of the Dioceses, Pastoral and Related Measures*, often referred to as the Toyne Review, provides some useful insights into this argument. The report explores the possibilities of validating new expressions of church within the legal structures of the Church of England. Paragraph 3.16 says: 'Our aim is to provide an overall framework within which diversity and complexity can be expressed. Being imaginative about new structures offers a means of protecting the parochial system in its widest sense.'[8]

It seems to me that the desire of the report is to provide ways of accommodating new expressions of church, which would naturally include the youth churches/congregations we have been discussing here, while at the same time preserving the legal structures of the Church of England. It is perhaps appropriate to hear what the Archbishop of Canterbury is quoted as saying in the report:

> at present there is actually an extraordinary amount going on in terms of the creation of new styles of church life. We can call it church planting, 'new ways of being church' or various other things; but the point is that more and more patterns of worship and shared life are appearing on the edge of our mainstream life that cry out for our support, understanding and nurture if they are not to get isolated and unaccountable.[9]

While we don't have space here for an in-depth exploration of the issues that this report presents, it is important to note that there is a good deal of will within the Church for new expressions of church to be encouraged and allowed to develop, while recognizing that there need to be sufficient levels of accountability and connection to the wider Church. The process that is emerging for this accountability and connection will probably take the form of new 'mission initiatives' (including youth churches/congregations) having to apply for a 'bishop's order', which will include a process of consultation and verification of the project. However, it must be stressed that at the time of writing, the General Synod of the Church of England is still reviewing this process.

'There is a good deal of will within the Church for new expressions of church to be encouraged and allowed to develop, while recognizing that there need to be sufficient levels of accountability and connection to the wider Church.'

Other considerations

It is well worth taking into consideration the long-term view of the proposed youth church/congregation. Is the aim of the project to feed young people into other, longer established churches containing a mix of ages, is it simply to allow the project to continue and become a young adult church or congregation, or do you have some other strategy in mind?

Prayer is, of course, an important activity throughout the whole process, as it is with any manifestation of church.

It is also worth asking what your relationship with other churches in your community will be. It may be that your youth congregation will attract young people from other churches. It is worth thinking about how you deal with this, before you experience it.

Thinking through the location of your meetings is important. Is it the best location for the people you are trying to reach? Regardless of whether we are trying to get away from the mainstream church in our approach or trying to foster healthy links, it's worth noting that most local churches sit in the heart of the community. If there are resources that the church can offer, then it could serve your purposes to use it as a base or meet within its vicinity. This could, however, detract from what you are trying to achieve.

The issue of when you will meet will obviously needs some thought. Many young people are regularly busy on Sunday mornings, and Sunday evenings can be difficult for those still in education preparing for the next day. It may be that a weekday evening is better or an after-school late afternoon slot.

Underpinning all the planning and preparation needs to be a sustained commitment to appropriate child protection policies and procedures. The necessary insurance and safety issues must be thought through and policies and procedures implemented. Good reference points for this information are AMAZE (whose web site is listed in the resources section at the end of the chapter) and your diocesan youth adviser or officer.

THINKING IT THROUGH

1. Is there a need for an expression of church specifically aimed at young people?
2. What other local provision is available for young people to access worship?
3. What links will you have to the local church and other churches in your area?
4. How will you develop a sacramental ministry with the young people?
5. What age of young people will you be targeting?
6. How will young people access what you do (practically – transport, time and venue)?
7. Are there other youth workers or church leaders in the area whom you could partner?
8. What is your long-term vision? For instance, what will happen when the young people get older – will you continue to meet and evolve the church/congregation with them or will they be encouraged to move to a different church to make way for a new generation of young people?

WHAT'S THE LINK BETWEEN 'YOUTH CHURCH' AND 'ADULT CHURCH'?

SUMMARY

It is my conviction that we are currently in state of flux with regards to the future of church and the debate about youth church and youth congregations is in the middle of that debate. It is also a very exciting time of innovation and change with more and more churches experimenting with ways of being church in order to meet the demands of declining church numbers and life in modern society. Risks need to be taken:

> In all probability many of our current forms and ways of being church will not prove adequate in the emerging society. It is young people whom we help to faith and equip to shape the emerging culture who will also need to develop new forms of worship and church structure which will one day be the mainstream.[10]

The results of risk taking are unknown and so what is required is openness and flexibility to the potential outcomes. As we have seen, it was the intention of some youth congregations to feed back into the mainstream church after a period of time. Some of these congregations became vibrant churches in themselves and the young people they sought to serve have grown up and they have become young

adult churches. Whether this is viewed as success or failure is secondary to the fact that a risk was taken, young people were reached and the dialogue about the future of church was developed further. Unity in the Church is a key issue and this will mean different things in different contexts, but ultimately there needs to be an increasing openness and flexibility in thinking about the ways of expressing church in order to maintain our alignment with God's mission in his world.

WHAT'S THE LINK BETWEEN 'YOUTH CHURCH' AND 'ADULT CHURCH'?

Web sites

www.alternativeworship.org
www.amaze.org.uk
www.emergingchurch.info

Books

Jonny Baker and Doug Gay, with Jenny Brown, *Alternative Worship*, SPCK, 2003.

Michael Frost and Alan Hirsch, *The Shaping of Things to Come*, Hendrickson, 2003.

Dan Kimball, *The Emerging Church: Vintage Christianity for new generations*, Zondervan, 2003.

NB The notes to this chapter refer to several books and web sites which, themselves, have useful Further Resources lists.

9 ALTERNATIVE FORMS OF WORSHIP

Pete Maidment

INTRODUCTION

The term 'alternative worship' elicits an interesting array of responses. For many, who take the title literally, the first question is often, 'Does that mean we're worshipping something alternative?' You can quickly see a look of fear enter their eyes as they contemplate worshipping some new God in some weird and wacky way. For those who have encountered alternative worship the response is usually one of two: if the experience had been a positive one, their eyes will light up as they recall the memory of something creative and exciting, something that drew them out of the humdrum of everyday life, into new and fascinating realms of God discovery; in others you will see a glazing over of the eyes as they picture a candle-lit room, filled with suffocating incense smoke and some dreary whale music on loop in the corner.

THE ISSUE: Alternative to what?

The term 'alternative worship' is probably a little bit misleading. It has been adopted as the name for much of the more reflective and creative worship that has been springing up in the Church since the mid 1990s. According to Jonny Baker and Doug Gay in their book *Alternative Worship*, the movement, in its purest form, offers 'new hopes for mission and church growth . . . at a time of crisis and decline in the mainstream denominations'.[1] They go on to explain the key characteristics of what has become known as the alternative worship movement:

- *dance*, and not just dance in the 'churchy dance' understanding, but rather an embracing of dance culture from clubs and raves;
- *pictures and images*, and in particular the use of electronic visuals and computer graphics as a means to enhance worship;
- *the ancient*, alternative worship has never been afraid to borrow from ancient spirituality and liturgy in juxtaposition to what it revels in from contemporary culture.

Baker and Gay believe that alternative worship is the closest the Church has come to a full exploration of what might be true postmodern worship.

The purpose of this chapter, rather than seeking to advocate one particular form of current worship practice, is to take a quick look at three emerging expressions of worship and to ask of each one what it can offer to the church seeking to help young people in their discovery of God through worship.

THEORY AND BACKGROUND: Why is alternative important?

For many young people, traditional church worship holds little or no interest any more, particularly in more evangelical churches where they can expect to have very little involvement with a service and a long un-interactive sermon. To them, the Church is quite simply no longer relevant. On the surface of it all, it may feel like a taste thing; the established or traditional church service no longer suits my taste and so I'll do something new. Jonny Baker admits to a little of this in the planning behind setting up Ealing's Grace congregation:

'For many young people, traditional church worship holds little or no interest any more.'

> The major motivation at that stage had been dissatisfaction, an increasing frustration at church culture which played music we'd never listen to at home, used language we wouldn't use anywhere else and served up a diet which had become over-familiar and often irrelevant.[2]

We mustn't, however, be fooled into thinking that taste is the only motivator behind the alternative worship movement. Paul Roberts warns us against the anger that can lie at the heart of such a 'revolutionary movement'.[3] Rather, the major motivation behind the alternative worship movement is cultural. When so much of the practice of the established Church is still rooted in modernity there must surely come an outlet for a more postmodern response to God. In his excellent booklet *Postmodern Culture and Youth Discipleship* Graham Cray notes that 'The postmodern age combines a spiritual hunger with a profound distrust of authoritative institutions, including religious ones'.[4] If the Church wants to reach a culture that is hungry for God but mistrusting of the institution then it must do something to bridge that gap. Where groups have sought to discover new forms of culturally relevant

'Where groups have sought to discover new forms of culturally relevant worship, without throwing out all that comes from the established Church, genuine growth occurs.'

worship, without throwing out all that comes from the established Church, genuine growth occurs.

It is of course also vital that we don't forget God's role in all of this: we mustn't be fooled into thinking that worship is something that we do to God. As stated in Chapter 1 of this book, worship is our response to God working in our lives, and the opportunity for us to come into his presence and receive from him.

It is difficult to ignore the fact that the Church generally is losing members, and particularly young members. The Church of England report *Mission-shaped Church* explains this in no uncertain terms and goes on to urge congregations to explore new forms of worship if they are to survive.[5] Paul Fiddes reminds us that true spiritual worship will be involved in the 'mission of God in the world'.[6] We must never forget that God is tirelessly seeking out the lost (Luke 15), and that his heart is decisively compassionate toward children (Mark 10.13–16).[7]

NEED TO KNOW: Three case studies

For many the question of where to start is the most terrifying. As discussed, alternative forms of worship don't have to mean new services or getting rid of pews. Alternative worship in this context is simply involving young people in the act of discovering God in their own settings and surroundings. The following three case studies offer three alternatives to the traditional church worship setting. I've tried to offer something to suit all tastes and hopefully something that will be useable in your situation. The examples have all started from one church or group. I haven't the space to talk about the impact of other worship movements or events (such as those connected with Iona, Taizé or Walsingham), but they are also worth a look at (see the 'Taking it further' section for more information). Please be aware that none of these can simply be cut and pasted into a new setting, they are all just ideas that others have tried and have worked. None of them is necessarily right or wrong: each one is simply one group's response to the challenge of worshipping God relevantly in this culture, seeking God's face, and sharing in his heart for mission.

'Alternative forms of worship don't have to mean new services or getting rid of pews. Alternative worship in this context is simply involving young people in the act of discovering God in their own settings and surroundings.'

CASE STUDY 1: Soul Survivor

It would be hard for me, impossible in fact, to do any case studies on forms of worship that have impacted youth ministry without taking a look at Soul Survivor. The fact that some of you are already thinking 'What's alternative about Soul Survivor?' only further proves that point. In some circles Soul Survivor has grown into the foremost worship festival for young people in this country and possibly worldwide. It has spawned a congregation in North London and has provided the model for much of the worship going on in youth groups around the country. For many involved in youth ministry, Soul Survivor no longer feels like an alternative form of worship, but rather the norm. A good number have taken their group to a Soul Survivor festival in Shepton Mallet, or have been to a Matt Redman or Tim Hughes gig; what's more, I'm sure that just as many have heard Mike Pilavachi speaking at one event or another.

'For many involved in youth ministry, Soul Survivor no longer feels like an alternative form of worship, but rather the norm.'

Soul Survivor started in the early 1990s when Mike Pilavachi, Soul Survivor's overall leader, then youth worker for St Andrew, Chorleywood, had a vision to lead an event for young people similar in nature to the already successful family event New Wine. Alongside one of his young people, Matt Redman, Mike had already started to discover something wonderful about worshipping together, simply praising God, praying, singing and reading the Word with nothing more than a guitar and a few voices. Mike writes that the vision for Soul Survivor is simple:

> The heart of it is to envision young people to capture first the vision of Jesus, and then his calling on their lives and then to equip them, train them and release them into ministry – so that they do it wherever they go, wherever they are.[8]

I'm sure that many of us at some point have bought a Soul Survivor worship book, dusted off the guitar, and jerkily strummed our way through the (mercifully simple) chords of Matt's latest song. But it just isn't the same: there's no way that any church can replicate the 'Soul Survivor experience'. The biggest impression that the attendee feels at the event is the passion and the power of the experience – there really is nothing to compare with the emotion felt when singing your heart out, joining together to lift Jesus' name on high.

So what is the alternative? Oddly enough, despite the vast nature of the Soul Survivor festival, the central theme, it would appear, to so many of the songs is intimacy. Soul Survivor's worship web site passionforyourname.com carries this quote from Sandy Millar: 'I would love to see a renewed energy going into writing simple, heartfelt intimate expressions of love.'[9] Despite the emphasis of a Soul Survivor festival on huge crowds and massive volume, the simple message about worship for the church or youth worker to take home, is that ultimately worship is about discovering an intimacy with Christ, at its heart worship is all about Jesus.

At a CYFA [Church Youth Fellowship Association] camp on the North Coast of Cornwall, the guy leading the sung worship was passionate about getting the young people involved in the worship in real depth, even so far as writing their own songs to fit the theme of the teaching (what Mike Pilavachi might call doing 'a new thing' in worship). It took only a little coaching from Duncan (the worship music leader) to see the young people producing their own, very powerful, worship songs, everything from 'classic' Soul Survivor style worship songs to a modern take on plainsong! One of the young people on the camp described it like this: 'It was different to singing a

Matt Redman song or a Soul Survivor song . . . it made you think much more, I listened to the words because I knew that he'd written them.'

So it really is achievable: all it takes is someone with a bit of music knowledge, plenty of prayer and the freedom to let yourself go! Soul Survivor grew out of two people, Matt and Mike, meeting weekly with a guitar and a Bible – it couldn't be simpler!

'It really is achievable: all it takes is someone with a bit of music knowledge, plenty of prayer and the freedom to let yourself go!'

CASE STUDY 2: Labyrinths and liquid worship

For many, however, the mere fact that worship is music or singing based is an instant turn-off. A complete opposite to the Soul Survivor model is the ancient practice of walking the labyrinth, which has been made popular again in recent years.

The labyrinth found new interest after a group of London's alternative worship communities created such an experience in St Paul's Cathedral as a way of celebrating the beginning of the twenty-first century. This labyrinth ritual combined the ancient practice of walking a path marked on the floor, with much more contemporary worship resources such as personal CD players, televisions and computers. Jonny Baker, one of the creators of the labyrinth makes this comment:

> It was a somewhat surprising sight to see artefacts of popular culture in the context of St Paul's Cathedral – flickering television screens, CD players and computers. It was the kind of art installation that would seem to have been more at home across the new millennium bridge on the other side of the Thames in the Tate Modern rather than in a traditional cathedral setting of Christian worship.[10]

The history of labyrinths is hard to trace. The earliest reference to one seems to be in the story of the Minotaur of Greek mythology. By today's definition, that would have been a maze as it almost certainly would have had dead ends and crossroads with choices of direction, whereas a true labyrinth today would be a winding single path that leads to a central point and then back out again. There are one entrance and one exit and no crossroads or dead ends.[11]

The power of a labyrinth is hard to explain; whether it's simply walking a route marked on the floor; following an interactive hi-tech labyrinth online; or just tracing the shape with your finger; something definitely happens. Perhaps it's just that in this busy world we take so little time out for quiet and reflection that the peace and tranquillity usually found in a labyrinth surprises and delights us.

'The power of a labyrinth is hard to explain; whether it's simply walking a route marked on the floor; following an interactive hi-tech labyrinth online; or just tracing the shape with your finger; something definitely happens.'

In turn labyrinths have led to an interest in a new kind of church service that feels much more 'liquid', which invites people to come and do whatever they feel like. When I was the leader of youth and children's work in Wonersh we used to run what we simply called 'Prayer and Praise Nights' with the 14- to 18-year-olds. The young people would decide on a theme and then we would divide the building we used into three parts. One room would be set up as a silent prayer room, with moving images, candles, soft music and dimmed lights. The young people would then deck the room out with Bible verses and thoughts to help the participants along in their prayer. Another room would be set up for music and singing, this room would have a CD player in it as well as a guitar and other musical instruments. Here the young people were free to worship God in the Soul Survivor style. A third room would be set up for 'prayer and toast'. This room was designed to look like a café with tables and chairs, a toaster and a kettle. Here the young people were encouraged to sit with food and drink and to pray for each other about issues covered in the silent prayer room or anything else they had on their hearts.

The key thing about both the labyrinth and liquid worship is that participants are allowed to go at their own pace. There's no 'president' who is keeping check on the time and rushing through a liturgy, but instead there is peace and God's time.

'The key thing about both the labyrinth and liquid worship is that participants are allowed to go at their own pace. There's no "president" who is keeping check on the time and rushing through a liturgy, but instead there is peace and God's time.'

Whatever you attempt, try giving the young people you are in contact with the opportunities to create their own worship space. Both labyrinths and liquid worship times have been a huge benefit to the groups I have worked with and both have provided some wonderful spiritually significant moments for those involved.

CASE STUDY 3: 24–7 prayer

If ever proof was needed that God is alive and kicking in the third millennium then the 24–7 prayer movement would seem to be it. Its story – growing from the vision of a little church in Chichester, on the south coast of England, to a global phenomenon – is nothing short of miraculous; with its effect no less dramatic.

The story began at the end of the last century when Pete Greig, one of the leaders at Revelation church in Chichester, felt called to lead his church in a prayer meeting that would last for 40 days, praying round the clock. They set aside a room in their church, filled it with loads of creative bits and bobs and went for it. Greig notes that even that first day seemed very hard, the few hours before midnight passing very slowly, but that by the time he returned at three in the morning the place was already buzzing.[12]

The vision of 24–7 is simple: that the only way that the Church will ever make an impact on the world is through prayer, and so we may as well pray hard: 24 hours a day, 7 days a week. Greig writes that '24–7 prayer exists to transform the world through a movement of Christ-centred and mission minded prayer.'[13]

'The vision of 24–7 is simple: that the only way that the Church will ever make an impact on the world is through prayer, and so we may as well pray hard: 24 hours a day, 7 days a week.'

If you are anything like me then the prospect of praying for a week, a night or even an hour is something pretty terrifying, and yet a 24–7 prayer room seems to break down those fears. It has to be experienced to be understood, but it is undoubtedly something amazing, which God very much has his hand on. Imagine the scene: you step into a room that looks completely crazy, there is paper everywhere: the walls are covered, the floor is swathed in the stuff, there's even a washing line hanging up with sheets of it pegged into position. The room has been divided up into sections, with sheets of material hanging from the ceiling and pinned to the walls. There are fairy lights twinkling from every available socket. There's a CD player in the corner that might be playing the most laid-back chill-out beats one minute and pumping worship the next. There are a couple of computers with the 24–7 web site on display.

What is most captivating, however, is that no matter what time of day (or night) you enter the room, you'll find that it's full of *prayer*. There are people young and old sitting quietly pouring their hearts out to God, or striding around the room calling out to their Father. Numerous pieces of paper are covered in scrawled prayer requests, for friends and relatives, people and places. Many of the sheets will have been filled out by passers-by as the intercessors went out onto the street to collect requests from shoppers during the day. The presence of God is truly palpable. It is the diversity of the content of a 24–7 prayer room that is so enchanting. If it was simply a ghetto for a bunch of Christians to hide in, then I suspect I would have no interest at all, but it is so much more.

First, it acts as a hub for mission: rarely will a 24–7 prayer room be filled just with Christians, rather it seems to draw all people to it. If peace is one of the greatest gifts that we have as followers of Christ, then perhaps nowhere will it be found more than in one of these prayer rooms. What's more, 24–7 has taken the prayer room all over the world, into desperate missionary situations in order to fulfil just that need. Greig writes at length about the impact that 24–7 had in Ibiza when it set up a prayer room there, praying for clubbers around the clock throughout the party season. Not just there, but in many eastern bloc countries throughout Europe and even as far away as communist China the 24–7 movement has brought its special brand of prayer-focused mission.

Taking up the challenge of setting up a 24–7 prayer room has two powerful effects on a church. First, it gets people praying and worshipping, and in a whole variety of ways. The prayer room urges you to experience God in new ways, whether through creativity, silence or mission. The other amazing effect of the prayer room is seeing the power of prayer on a church.

'The prayer room urges you to experience God in new ways, whether through creativity, silence or mission. The other amazing effect of the prayer room is seeing the power of prayer on a church.'

There's too much to write about 24–7 in one small chapter, I urge you to at the very least check out the web site and even better to read some of the books about the movement in the 'Taking it further' section below.

THINKING IT THROUGH

Perhaps you might find these questions helpful as you assess what more you could do with the worship in your church:

1. How involved are your young people with the planning and delivery of worship in either the main church services or in their youth group?
2. When was the last time you did something alternative in your main worship service?
3. Are your young people engaged with the worship at your church or do they find it unhelpful or, worse, plain boring?

ALTERNATIVE FORMS OF WORSHIP

SUMMARY

As I've already written, none of these ideas is designed to be picked up and transplanted into your setting. Instead they are here to challenge you into thinking about the context your work with young people exists in, and to try to make the worship that is on offer to them fit it.

ALTERNATIVE FORMS OF WORSHIP

In this final section you will find a wealth of resources available to you to help you be more creative with your worship.

Soul Survivor

The best place to look for information about Soul Survivor is their web site www.soulsurvivor.com. Here you'll find information on training and teaching, as well as links to their online shop where you can buy books and so forth. Soul Survivor also run their own site devoted entirely to worship www.passionforyourname.com. Other sites worth checking out are www.mattredman.com and www.worshiptogether.com.

Labyrinths and liquid worship

To try out a labyrinth for yourself visit www.yfc.co.uk/labyrinth, this is a virtual version of the labyrinth that was set up and run in St Paul's Cathedral in 2000. For more info on the history of labyrinths have a look at www.labyrinthsociety.org (note that it isn't a Christian site but has some good information). Just doing an image search for 'labyrinth' on Google usually brings up some good sites as well. The following books are worth looking at:

Sally Dakin and Ian Tarrant, *Labyrinths and Prayer Stations*, Grove Books, 2004.

Tim Lomax and Michael Moynagh, *Liquid Worship*, Grove Books, 2004.

24–7 prayer

Much the same as Soul Survivor, the best place to look for more info here is the movement web site: www.24–7prayer.com. Here you'll find links to all of the places that are currently praying, as well as all the resources that 24–7 have published and made available. I can't recommend the book to you enough *Red Moon Rising* by Pete Greig and Dave Roberts (Kingsway, 2004), it's awesome!

General alternative worship resources

The following are good places to look for more information about alternative worship.

Books

Jonny Baker and Doug Gay, with Jenny Brown, *Alternative Worship*, SPCK, 2003.

Tony Jones, *Soul Shaper: Exploring spirituality and contemplative practices in youth ministry*, Zondervan, 2004.

In line with contemporary culture, most of the best alternative worship resources can be found online, the following is by no means an exhaustive list:

www.alternativeworship.org

www.freshworship.org – The links section here is awesome.

www.rejesus.co.uk

www.osbd.org – One Small Barking Dog, the resources section here is well worth a visit.

Other worship events or places that have an impact on young people and would be seen as alternative include:

The Taizé Community: www.taize.fr

Walsingham Youth Pilgrimage: www.walsinghamanglican.org.uk/education/

The Iona Community: www.iona.org.uk

SPIRITUALITY

In this section David Brown explores what we mean by the spirituality of young people and suggests ways in which you can engage with it and help them to develop a truly Christian spirituality.

10 WHAT DO WE MEAN BY 'SPIRITUALITY'?

David Brown

INTRODUCTION

Every so often, a new phrase or buzzword percolates to the top of youth-work practice, causing much debate, sometimes quite a bit of heat, and occasionally some light! One such word that has recently generated debate both within the Christian youth ministry sector and the statutory youth-work context has been 'spirituality'. In particular there has been a great deal of debate about how the concepts of spirituality and 'spiritual development' relate to young people.[1]

This chapter seeks in oh-so-few words, to point out *some* thinking (note my italics), on the following:

- the nature of human spirituality;
- the nature of youth work, young people and spiritual development;
- the practice of youth work as a spiritual discipline.

It is my intention that 'spirituality' becomes a word that you, the reader, will feel more able to engage with – even if that means the quotation marks around spirituality are noted, explored, described and questioned!

THEORY AND BACKGROUND

Let us look at the theory and the background of spirituality.

The nature of human spirituality

According to Brown and Furlong, spirituality is a 'weasel word', hard to spot and even harder to catch![2] Christian for his part, writes that 'The very nature of the subject [spirituality] makes it speculative, unsuitable for empirical tests, which produce irrefutable, or at least replicable results.'[3]

However, while the notion of spirituality might be difficult to define, each of us, whether religious or not, experiences the spiritual.

Some views on spirituality

Rolheiser notes that spirituality is 'about what we do with our unrest', in that, as Jung articulated, everyone is 'overcharged' with an energy for life 'that structures our souls and imperialistically demands our every attention'.[4] Discussing spirituality therefore is about what, and who, we are as human beings, that is, what drives us.

'Spirituality therefore is about what, and who, we are as human beings, that is, what drives us.'

The psychologist Maslow in his now famous theory on human motivation, noted that as humans we are controlled by a series of 'drives' starting with our physiological needs eventually culminating in the meeting of what he referred to as our need for self-actualization.[5] While Maslow's theory on human development has been often critiqued, the idea of becoming self-actualized or, it might be argued, spiritually complete remains a persuasive idea prominent within the liberal, humanistic view of spirituality.

The theologian John Macquarrie, for his part, while acknowledging that 'spirituality' has become a term of 'doubtful repute', does within one sentence encapsulate usefully what this word might mean: 'Spirituality has to do with becoming a person in the fullest sense.'[6]

Macquarrie's thinking on the fulfilment of human experience as becoming followers of Christ echoes Jesus' words to those who would follow: 'I have come that you might have life and life to the full' (John 10.10 NIV).

The nature of youth work, young people and spiritual development

Leighton in his seminal work *The Principles and Practice of Youth and Community Work* believes that youth work is not only a philosophical exercise (that is, an enquiry into the nature of things), but (and these are his words) 'an exercise of faith'.[7] Treating the work as an exercise of faith therefore (and despite the male pronoun):

> The youth worker must believe that he is engaged in a relationship which enables young people to discover the something that one must get out of life. But he also believes that some forms of life are better than others, that health is preferred to sickness, education to ignorance, freedom to bondage.[8]

Could it therefore be argued that youth work is spiritual in that it is about young people discovering 'the something' they must get out of life? Even if, this something is not clearly defined, leaving it elusive and ephemeral?

'Could it therefore be argued that youth work is spiritual in that it is about young people discovering "the something" they must get out of life? Even if, this something is not clearly defined, leaving it elusive and ephemeral?'

Young argues passionately that if youth work is to remain true to its calling, the profession must open up fundamental philosophical questions around its nature and purpose. One might argue that in doing so, youth work becomes a spiritual activity: 'Exploring values is therefore not a part of youth work. It is all of youth work. It is the very foundation of the work and this is what makes youth work an exercise in moral philosophy.'[9]

I would strongly echo this sentiment particularly in regard to the nature of spirituality within youth work not least (but maybe above all) because young people themselves are spiritual.

Young people and spirituality

One of my most harrowing experiences as a youth worker was in supporting a youth club member through the death of her younger brother due to a severe asthma attack.

The young woman's questions and those of her peer group who formed the youth project I worked alongside were searching, troubling and primarily concerned with finding some meaning or purpose in the midst of this tragedy. Young people have a right to ask existential questions, as they make sense of their world and place in it, and often direct and difficult experiences fuel this awareness and search. Youth workers (if spiritually aware) are divinely placed to respond.

I have shared a personal story on one aspect of a young person's articulation of their awareness and questioning of what is beyond them, as it opens up the discussion of young people and their sense of what is spiritual. Wyn and White, for example, put forward a relatively orthodox view that young people 'construct' a sense of their identity through various social interactions, at home, at school, with peers, and so on.[10] They quote from the work of Wexler who develops a theory around adolescence not only in terms of young people 'finding themselves' but also of their 'becoming somebody'. The concept of becoming somebody ought to include how young people deal with life (in its fullest sense), including that which is beyond them, the transcendent, or we could state the 'spiritual'.

It can be argued that in becoming somebody, young people do engage with issues and phenomena that are existential in nature. Hay and Nye provide strong evidence for this. In their seminal work on children and spirituality, they propose that spirituality comes out of direct experience. As such, children's expressions of their sense of the spiritual have three interrelated themes:

- awareness of the here and now;
- awareness of mystery;
- awareness of value.[11]

It does not take much imagination to transfer these categories to our understanding of young people's spirituality. A word of caution, however. While I have articulated a view that young people have a spiritual element to their nature, this may not be what young people themselves consider as important or relevant! It seems that an awareness of one's 'inner being' only comes through experience and, vitally, reflection on it.

If Hay and Nye provide a thematic model of the spirituality of young people, then the National Youth Agency's *National Occupational Standards for Youthwork* has sought to label aspects of spiritual development for youth work professionals.[12] Interestingly, under Element B.2.2 of the *Occupational*

Standards, youth work as a profession is encouraged to have a view to 'enabling young people to have a sense of and value their life journey', of which the following aspects or traits of spirituality are noted, 'wonder, acceptance, compassion, integrity, commitment, curiosity'.

The explicit understanding therefore behind this section of the *Occupational Standards for Youthwork* is to encourage young people and youth-work practitioners to develop their 'spiritual self' including the above attributes. The question remains . . . How?

NEED TO KNOW: The practice of youth work as a spiritual discipline

You may well at this point be wondering what all of this discussion around young people and their awareness of the spiritual has to do with the local youngsters who hang out at the bottom of the street? What relevance has 'becoming a person in the fullest sense' got to do with teenage issues such as school, family, peers, the latest mobile phone, and watching the current round of *Big Brother* evictions?

Let me try and offer some signposts.

1. Young people have a 'spiritual default setting'

The laptop that I am currently using comes with many features, some of which I will probably never need! However, while I can change aspects of my computer and how it operates, it will always carry the pre-programmed default settings that the makers installed for how the computer best runs. When I mess up some aspect of the computer's configuration, the default settings allow me to return to the PC's best operating status.

Despite all classifications that society seeks to put on the young, young people are at their very core spiritual. This is their default setting. They may not be overtly aware that this is the case, nor indeed may some who work alongside them, but each individual young person you encounter carries what Parsons calls the 'spark of the divine'.[13] The Scriptures tell us that 'God

'Young people are at their very core spiritual. This is their default setting.'

spoke: "Let us make human beings in our image, make them reflecting our nature" ' Genesis 1.26 (*The Message*).

The spark of the divine is in knowing that we are made in God's image. (This, might I add, is one of the significant differences between a Christian-based understanding of spirituality and a more secular viewpoint). Youth work, or as it is becoming more commonly known youth ministry, across the Church, is the living out of this default setting, acknowledging our beginning and ending in God the creator. Youth ministry ought to allow God's nature to be reflected, experienced and shared with and between this generation of young people. This is the underpinning to all we do with young people, and all we are as leaders to those we seek to accompany.

'Youth ministry ought to allow God's nature to be reflected, experienced and shared with and between this generation of young people. This is the underpinning to all we do with young people, and all we are as leaders to those we seek to accompany.'

2. Being 'spiritual' is about the ordinary

Practically speaking, however, supporting young people as they develop a deepening awareness of the God who loves and has created them is a very ordinary activity. Christian spirituality at its core is about the ordinary stuff of life. The ordinary stuff being wrapped up in the love and reality of Jesus Christ . . . and the corresponding demands that this love makes on us!

For those of us who work with young people, being authentically spiritual means being authentically real. Teaching the Christian faith in twenty-first-century Britain and Ireland is very much about living the faith – and being somewhat vulnerable about how we as youth ministers work out the spiritual issues confronting and exciting us. The welcomed growth in professionalism across the Church in terms of youth work can never replace genuine, warm, open and Christian relationships with today's teenager.

'The welcomed growth in professionalism across the Church in terms of youth work can never replace genuine, warm, open and Christian relationships with today's teenager.'

These relationships make real the spiritual aspect of life, and need to include the awe-inspiring and the mundane of human existence. These relationships ought to make for life-changing discipleship, for us and those we minister with, through the *inspiration* of God's Holy Spirit.

3. The role of the Church

It is rather too easy at this point simply to note how irrelevant the Church has become for most young people. Anecdotal evidence and a plethora of research initiatives across the United Kingdom and Ireland would evidence the falling out between the institution of the Church and many of our young. As people involved in youth ministry we see this phenomenon, and sometimes empathize with it!

However, I am by no means suggesting that the Church has lost the plot entirely when it comes to engaging spiritually with teenagers and young adults. Where young people are welcomed into the community of faith, where their life and energy is nurtured and where a Christian faith tradition is embraced wholeheartedly, deep spiritual needs are met.

'Where young people are welcomed into the community of faith, where their life and energy is nurtured and where a Christian faith tradition is embraced wholeheartedly, deep spiritual needs are met.'

The Christian Church in its breadth of tradition, worship experience and spirituality *has* ample resources at its disposal in the work of God's kingdom among our young. A key question remains, do we actually believe and practise 'wholeheartedly' our Christian tradition? If we come from a liturgical/sacramental tradition, are these elements practised well? If our worship style is full of energy, charismatic and noisy or quiet and contemplative, are young people drawn to participate by the reality of these worship traditions? For all the negative press the Church gets today, Christian spirituality is based on the premise that we are made to belong together. It is wrong to claim to follow Christ and yet to seek to embrace a 'Lone Ranger spirituality' (to go it alone)!

THINKING IT THROUGH

1. How would you describe 'spirituality'?
2. What differences are there between religion and spirituality?
3. If spirituality is about the here and now, value and mystery,[14] how can these factors become a reality in our youth ministry?
4. What practices do we as Christians utilize that express the spiritual?

WHAT DO WE MEAN BY 'SPIRITUALITY'?

SUMMARY

Part of my frustration in writing this piece has been my overwhelming desire to give advice on 'how to work with young people spiritually'. As if spirituality, let alone Christian spirituality, can be reduced to an Ikea flat-pack instruction leaflet! (A follows B which then leads to C . . .)

For some, a sense of that which is spiritual will always be tied in to the institution of the Church. Increasingly for others, an awareness of the spiritual side of life requires a secular or non-religious approach. Postmodernity, it seems, offers spiritual choice, which suits today's 'seeker' outlook, but may not shape the spirit.

Talking about spirituality requires openness to the whole of our human experience: the awe, wonder, mystery, and as I have noted above – the ordinary! It is time that those of us who claim the name of Christ, embody the depth and reality of his life, words and example. Giving body to the spiritual is our vocation.

WHAT DO WE MEAN BY 'SPIRITUALITY'?

A. Brown and J. Furlong, *Spiritual Development in Schools*, second edn, National Society, 1997.

D. Hay and R. Nye, *The Spirit of the Child*, HarperCollins, 1998.

J. P. Leighton, *The Principles and Practice of Community Youthwork*, second edn, Chester House, 1975.

J. Macquarrie, *Paths in Spirituality*, SCM Press, 1972.

A. H. Maslow, *Motivation and Personality*, Harper and Row, 1987.

National Youth Agency, *National Occupational Standards for Youthwork*, January 2000.

L. Parsons, 'Youth work and the spark of the divine', 2002. Downloadable from www.infed.org/christianyouthwork/spark_of_the_divine.htm, or available in print from Publications, YMCA George Williams College, 199 Freemasons Road, Canning Town, London E16 3PY.

R. Rolheiser, *Seeking Spirituality*, Hodder & Stoughton, 1998.

R. White and J. Wyn, *Rethinking Youth*, Sage, 1997.

K. Young, *The Art of Youthwork*, Russell House, 1999.

M. Green, 'Spirituality', *Youth and Policy*, Issue 65, National Youth Agency, 1999.

11 DEVELOPING A CHRISTIAN SPIRITUALITY WITH YOUNG PEOPLE

David Brown

INTRODUCTION

If we as youth ministers believe that God impacts young people, then it is for us to help create (with them), the 'sacred space' within which they will encounter the living God. This sacred space or living awareness of God and the discipline of discovering this, will mean different things for different young people. Our responsibility is to faithfully and diligently serve our young people . . . knowing that ultimately all ministry is not ours but Christ's.

> I'm not praying for the God-rejecting world
> But for those you gave me,
> *For they are yours by right.*
>
> John 17.9 (*The Message*, my italics)

NEED TO KNOW: Practising the presence of God – some 'how tos'

These suggestions are divided into two sections: 'Getting away from it all' includes one-off or special events beyond the church walls. The second section looks at how we can encourage young people to develop spiritual disciplines in their everyday lives.

GETTING AWAY FROM IT ALL

Pilgrimage

Undoubtedly one of the most important metaphors for the Christian life down through the years has been that of the pilgrimage or journey. Travelling a pilgrimage requires planning and preparation, a sense of hopefulness and anticipation about the destination (in most cases), and yet nervousness about what might lie ahead.

The British Isles are blessed with numerous places of pilgrimage: Iona in Scotland, Walsingham, England, and of course in Ireland, Knock Mountain, or Glendalough. Many young people over the years have also visited the Taizé Community in France.

At many levels of a young person's experience, a pilgrimage can be a life-changing experience. Young people are drawn out of their comfort zone and maybe for the first time encouraged really to rely on God and others. Travelling to a place where prayer and worship are placed centre stage in the life of a community can place in context the busyness of life at home. Being thrust into a community of prayer, and following a rule of life, speaks volumes into the soul. Many of us, unused to such daily discipline may well find such a prayer routine and discipline a shock to the system. In many ways, if handled with discernment and reassurance, this is no bad thing for a young person to experience.

'A pilgrimage can be a life-changing experience. Young people are drawn out of their comfort zone and maybe for the first time encouraged really to rely on God and others.'

Practically speaking, a journey can bring out the best and worst in a group of young people. Tiredness, irritability and personality conflicts can come to the fore. The group (or individual) naturally will experience the highs and lows of the pilgrimage. It is all worth it, however, as making pilgrimage together is one way to allow sacred space to occur. Iona, for example, has been called a 'thin place' – thin in so far as the world we inhabit and the eternal world to come are almost within touching distance.

If possible, go on pilgrimage yourself to Iona, Taizé or wherever seems appropriate. Not only will your trip allow you first-hand experience of the journey physically and spiritually, but you too might be surprised by what surprises you! Pilgrimage, it has to be said, is experiential learning for your young people with walking boots on!

Do a labyrinth

Based closely on the model of pilgrimage, the last few years have seen a revival of a medieval Christian tradition known as the labyrinth (Pete Maidment also describes this in Chapter 9). A labyrinth, like the pilgrimage, reflects one's journey throughout life with God. Unlike a pilgrimage that requires travelling to a destination, completing a labyrinth requires one (for it is primarily a solitary journey) to travel a set pattern, usually laid out in front of you.

Thankfully, a few years ago British Youth for Christ had the impulse to re-work the labyrinth idea for people today. The same journey is walked, but at various points along the way, prayer stations are used. The walkers wear personal headsets, and a gentle voice guides them along the labyrinth, requiring them to stop, pray, reflect, and so on.

The exciting thing about labyrinth is that holy space is created wherever the labyrinth is set up. That might be a cathedral, a school hall, a prison gym. The possibilities are endless. Surprisingly for a generation that thrives on background noise, many young people genuinely appreciate an opportunity to be quiet, and to be led. The labyrinth's success (if success is the right word) is in the fact that individuals find their own level with God as they walk the pattern. You are allowed room to be spiritual, in touch and in tune.

'Surprisingly for a generation that thrives on background noise, many young people genuinely appreciate an opportunity to be quiet, and to be led.'

One word of caution that needs articulating at this point. For some young people, irrespective of background, doing a labyrinth or going on a pilgrimage may be something that deeply moves or shocks them – emotionally and spiritually. If both practices mirror life's journey, then for some this will be a difficult one. It is essential that there should be men and women of, let's say, Christian maturity around as the young people engage in these spiritual disciplines – if only to aid the young people as they reflect on the experience they have just had.

The outdoor environment

In Chapter 10 I noted that Hay and Nye put forward the idea that spirituality in part is comprised of 'awe and wonder'. Unfortunately for many of us, the sense of awe and wonder can often elude our shrink-wrapped, neatly packaged world. Then a tsunami hits the coast of Sri Lanka, or a hurricane floods New Orleans.

There is little doubt that we as created beings (Genesis 1) often come to our senses when confronted by the power and might of creation. We are not ultimately in control. We are best to keep quiet and offer due praise and adoration to the one who creates and sustains.

While there are real dangers in exploring the outdoor environment, and all possible practical and professional precautions need to be taken into account, one sure way to allow young people a sense of the eternal and to experience God is through exposure to the outside world. Throughout the history of British and Irish youth work, the role of outdoor education has been linked to the social development of young people. However, when the theories have passed away, and the life skills have been learned (important as they are), the outdoor world reminds us that 'The earth is the Lord's and all that is in it' (Psalm 24.1).

Without being oversimplistic, at every level of a young person's experience, time in the natural world awakens the senses to awe, wonder, mystery, and responsibility for the created world. Christian youth ministry above all has a unique gift to offer today's young people in pointing to the creator of the cosmos, and reminding them that they too, are made in the creator's image.

Up until this point, we have been focusing on how Christian spirituality can be experienced or practised by, in one sense, intentionally getting away from it all. Indeed in the story from Acts 8 where Philip meets the Ethiopian Eunuch, the 'conversion' of the Ethiopian courtier could only have happened because both men were in a different place from normal and, let's say, more receptive to the Holy Spirit's work. Their encounter changed both lives, but it occurred far from home.

DEVELOPING SPIRITUAL DISCIPLINES IN EVERYDAY LIFE

Christian spirituality, or the work of God in our lives is nothing if not about the everyday. If the story of Jesus, his life, death and resurrection is to have any meaning for young people, then it has to be about their (indeed our) everyday reality. We as Christian youth ministers need to get across the message that maintaining a spiritual life is about spiritual *practice* and *discipline*. Here are a few practices that might allow that God reality to evolve.

> **'Christian spirituality, or the work of God in our lives is nothing if not about the everyday.'**

The quiet time

While for some evangelicals the notion of a daily quiet time conjures up memories of not being very disciplined in the past, a daily routine that seeks to build in time with the Bible has to be a no-brainer in terms of developing a disciplined spiritual life. The Christian market is today flooded with study aids, student Bibles, and web-based resources, designed to aid teens in their search after God. All of this is very welcome. Remember though that many young people from a non-book culture may well struggle in reading and digesting God's word – especially if it feels like a series of study questions will follow. Ultimately whatever tool or resource is used in opening up God's word for reflection, the best guide for a young person will be your own experience. While the quiet time may today seem very countercultural, creating time to be quiet before God's word allows his Spirit a chance to speak, and for us to respond.

Lectio Divina

Akin to the quiet time is the practice from the Benedictines whereby reading God's word and being still with it, creates room for the Word of God to speak directly to the heart. Clearly Bible study aids are hugely important when it comes to developing a deeper understanding of God's word. However, the practice of *Lectio Divina* allows the Scriptures to speak for themselves. Prayer, meditation and contemplation on God's word, can allow for the presence of Christ to become real. Above all *Lectio Divina* calls young people to hear God's voice, to sense his presence and to respond. The Irish Jesuit web site, www.sacredspace.ie gives daily *Lectio Divina* readings that might be useful to some young people

Prayer

It feels somewhat disparaging to the breath of life that is prayer for the Christian to offer a few sentences. Suffice to say, that the more creative we can be in teaching prayer to and with young people, the better! Experience dictates that prayer, be it formally led from a pulpit or screamed out in private, ought to be honest. Young people who intuitively know the real thing, are drawn to the reality of prayer whether they experience contemplative prayer amidst several thousand at Taizé or Charismatic intercessory prayer within a local youth cell group. The Hebrew tradition of praying through the Psalms as our Lord did, surely models the hurt, anger, joy, praise, loneliness and trust that a genuine experience of prayer draws us into. Again, if in youth ministry leadership, our struggles and joy in praying are shared, young people are allowed permission to find their language and their way into Christ's arms.

> **'Experience dictates that prayer, be it formally led from a pulpit or screamed out in private, ought to be honest. Young people who intuitively know the real thing, are drawn to the reality of prayer whether they experience contemplative prayer amidst seven thousand at Taizé or Charismatic intercessory prayer within a local youth cell group.'**

THINKING IT THROUGH

1. It is easy to see youth ministry as being what 'we do' with young people. What does it mean to take Christ at his word and see young people as God's work, not ours? (See John 17)
2. The theme of journeying is a constant metaphor throughout the Scriptures describing how God relates to us. How best might we journey with today's teenagers, and invite them to be part of our own spiritual journeying?
3. It has been said that you can only lead someone to where you are and no further. If that's true, what sort of spiritual discipline ought to shape our awareness of God within and around us?
4. How do we share in practice the astounding fact that Christ is interested in our everyday reality with young people?
5. When, where and how did you last encounter Christ?

DEVELOPING A CHRISTIAN SPIRITUALITY WITH YOUNG PEOPLE

SUMMARY

It has been a struggle writing a more practical 'how to' guide to developing young people and their Christian spirituality. Not because 2,000 years of Christian history have proven these practices as being invalid, but rather because the only way a young person will know that Christ lives is when we likewise practise the presence of Christ, becoming authentic witnesses to his life and love. Youth ministry ought to be a tough call, not due to the nature of today's teenagers but because of the privilege and responsibility of living as authentic followers of Christ among the young God has called us to serve.

If Christian youth work or ministry is to impact today's teenager in praxis, then it cannot avoid the ordinary stuff of life that makes up their and *our* lives. It is this ordinary stuff that we know God breathes life into, to his glory. Developing with our young people practices that lead to lifelong discipleship and nurture Christian spirituality ought to be at the forefront of youth ministry at the start of this millennium.

Go practise!!

DEVELOPING A CHRISTIAN SPIRITUALITY WITH YOUNG PEOPLE

Web sites

The Taizé Community: www.taize.fr

Walsingham Youth Pilgrimage: http://www.walsinghamanglican.org.uk/education/

The Iona Community: www.iona.org.uk

Lectio Divina: www.sacredspace.ie
www.labyrinth.org.uk/

Books

S. Case, *God Is Here: Connecting with Him in Everyday Life*, Relevant Books, 2005.

Andy Flannagan, *God 360*, Authentic Media Publishing, 2006.

K. Lake, *Reunderstanding Prayer: A fresh approach to conversation with God*, Relevant Books, 2005.

M. Yaconelli, *Contemplative Youth Ministry: Practicing the presence of Jesus with young people*, SPCK, 2006.

POSTSCRIPT: Is Sunday linked with Monday?

Mark Montgomery

INTRODUCTION

At the start of the book we defined worship as:

> what happens when we are conscious of God and long to be closer to him. Worship is standing before God and learning how to live. Worship is that 'yes' which is our heartfelt and instinctive response to the God who made us and loves us and died for us, who lives for us and in us.

If it is the case that worship is 'standing before God and learning how to live', why is it that so many young people (and adults) think of worship as something that only happens on a Sunday? In this chapter, we are going to look at how we can encourage young people to worship God throughout the week and their entire lives.

THE ISSUE

The church I worshipped in as a teenager had quite a large youth group, about 30 of us. That translated to a regular (three out of four Sundays) church attendance of around twelve, which rose and fell depending on circumstances and events. This, I believe, was pretty good: I knew that there were churches that had larger church attendance from their youth groups and there were those that had less. However, looking at those friends I used to attend church with, and considering those who are still involved in regularly attending church today, the numbers significantly change. Out of those 30 members of the youth group I can name only a handful of friends who still attend church ever, and out of the twelve there are only about six who have regular involvement with a church today. So why is this?

For me there is a deeper issue, which is not just about how we link Sunday to Monday but how we help young people into a worshipping faith that they own for a lifetime. Encouraging young people to 'stand before God and learn how to live' for the rest of their lives, in all the situations they face (good and bad), I believe is the key in helping them to link their Sunday and

Monday experiences. I am going to draw on my own faith journey and my experience as a youth worker to help us think through the issues involved in helping young people who are conscious of God to stand before him and learn how to live.

'Encouraging young people to "stand before God and learn how to live" for the rest of their lives, in all the situations they face (good and bad), I believe is the key in helping them to link their Sunday and Monday experiences.'

THEORY AND BACKGROUND

When we open up the issue of how we link Sunday to Monday, we have to look at the wider issue of how to engage young people in a faith that they own for their lives and not just how we bridge the gap between the Sunday and mid-week experiences. In helping young people to develop their faith we need to know something of the culture that the young people live in and thus the culture we want to engage with. There are plenty of books available to help you understand youth culture and current trends (see 'Taking it further' on p. 145), so I am not going to go into detail here. I will, however, make some brief comments on the world in which young people live, to help us think around the subject of encouraging young people into lifelong worship.

The world that young people now live in is generally a completely different place to where most of us grew up. A couple of the main changes are choice and participation, and these are key factors when thinking of how we link Sunday to Monday.

Choice

Young people have more choice, and more power to make choices, than they have had for many generations. The last 20 years have seen the growth of marketing targeted specifically at children and young people, the growth in digital technology (the many different activities young people can engage with now, such as computer games consoles, DVDs, computers, etc.) and more spending power available to them. Choice is all around them. This choice is also translated into the education system: there are many more subjects to choose from at GCSE, A level and degree level than there were ten years ago, for example. This choice creates pressure on young people to conform to peers', parents' and society's expectations.

In other areas of their lives, young people are presented with a myriad of options from which to choose: what activities to participate in outside school, where to go and what to do at the weekend, which channels to watch on TV (or whether to watch a DVD or play a computer game instead), which magazines and blogs to read, what camps or activities to participate in over the summer holiday, what to do with their gap year – the list goes on. Many of us may think we had all these choices to make too, so what has changed? But young people now have many more choices to make than we ever had. Church – if and where and when to go – is just one of those choices.

Participation

In terms of youth work one of the key areas that the government has been focused on in recent years is young people's participation in the decision-making process. Encouraging participation is also one of the key emphases of youth work as set out by the *National Occupational Standards for Youth Work*.[1] Most young people love to be involved in setting up and running projects, and this encourages ownership. This is also recognized in the education field by the rise in new teaching methods and school councils. Again, this is a significant change in young people's lives: no longer are they just 'recipients' and 'taught', but they have active opportunities to shape their experiences.

Unfortunately churches have lagged behind the education system in many respects. Many young people see church as something that is done to them, rather than them actually owning the experience. I would argue that this is one of the main reasons why many young people love going to youth groups and youth services but hardly ever turn up to regular worship times, as they are not allowed or encouraged to have any real participation in them. In this book we have tried to help you think through ways of addressing that situation.

> **'Churches have lagged behind the education system in many respects. Many young people see church as something that is done to them, rather than them actually owning the experience.'**

Many young people now don't have their church involvement handed down to them, as their parents don't go to church, so church is normally something they choose to participate in as one of the many activities that they might be involved with. As church or youth group is just one of the many activities in which young people may be involved, it may take them time to understand and commit to a real living faith. We cannot necessarily speed up their process of commitment as that is in God's hands. However, we can put into place opportunities for them to meet with God. This, however, is difficult to achieve if we limit those opportunities to just a couple of hours one night a week.

NEED TO KNOW: Four key principles

Having thought about the world we are engaging in there are four principles for the Church and young people that we need to address and incorporate into our work with young people. Keeping these at the core of our work will help young people have a lifelong worshipping faith. The first three issues we need to focus on are relationships, ownership and freedom; all are within the context of the fourth. Let's explore them a little.

Relationships

For me relationships were key in my faith development, especially as I started to form my own ideas, question and understand my faith. These were significant relationships, not just friendships, they were the relationships that challenged and pushed me. I suppose you would probably call these people my mentors, or people who have accompanied me on my journey.[2] These were people who put time into me and were there when I needed them to be. Don't get me wrong: they weren't on call twenty-four/seven but always made the time to help me grapple with the tough issues. If you think back in your faith journey you can probably recognize similar people. These relationships are key in helping young people develop their faith and link the Sunday experience to the rest of their life.

You are probably now thinking 'How can I make those relationships when there are many different young people in the church?' Let's reflect about how Jesus did it. Out of the many Jesus chose twelve to spend time with and out of those twelve he picked three with whom he developed significant relationships (Peter, James and John). We have to remember that the mentoring of young people isn't just down to the youth leaders – it should be a whole-church activity. Let the young people choose those they want to mentor them: you might be surprised by whom they pick. When we develop these relationships we have to remember child protection guidelines and also that it is all about helping the young people discover their faith. We should meet the young people where they are at and not try to enforce our world view on to them. As said earlier, they must make their own choices. If faith is to be nurtured and developed, then relationships are fundamental to everything.[3]

'The mentoring of young people isn't just down to the youth leaders – it should be a whole-church activity.'

Ownership

How can young people link Sunday to Monday if they don't own their faith? Young people need to understand what they are saying and doing when they sit in church. We should not assume that because we understand a particular way of doing things the young people do. If young people don't understand their faith how are they meant to own it? Churches have the idea that if people are attending church and other activities they have a growing and lifelong faith. In some cases this is true, but when we think of young people this might not be the case. We shouldn't confuse participation with ownership. In my experience and as can be seen with the drop-off of young people in the church, some young people attend youth club and church on a Sunday simply as one of their hobbies. We should also not assume that because a young person is growing up in a Christian home they have their own faith. As commented earlier, young people won't engage with a handed-down faith. Gavin Calver, in *Disappointed with Jesus*, comments 'they need to own their faith, develop in it, and grow. Inherited faith is a waste of time.'[4]

Authentic participation is key in this area. Allowing young people to interact, form questions and have a hands-on role in services, youth clubs and other activities will help them understand, and then over time, own their faith. It is important that you don't just pay lip-service to the young people and involve them in lesser roles, but actually give them the opportunity to fully participate with issues that affect them. 'The key must be that they make their own choices and draw their own conclusions.'[5] Throughout this book you have many examples of how this can be done.

'Allowing young people to interact, form questions and have a hands-on role in services, youth clubs and other activities will help them understand, and then over time, own their faith.'

Freedom

If we are going to give young people authentic participation then we need to give young people two types of freedom, and this is where it gets difficult. The first, allowing young people the freedom to express themselves in worship, can be quite difficult for churches. This type of freedom may

'Allowing young people the freedom to express themselves in worship, can be quite difficult for churches.'

threaten traditions in the church and challenge an established way of doing things, but it is something we need to do. Young people are creative and energetic by nature and this can have a very positive effect on the church. This type of freedom can allow young people also to explore vocations in terms of ministry. If young people haven't tried something how are they meant to know if it's what God wants them to do? We should also offer young people the freedom to explore different faith opportunities and experiences. We should actively participate in helping them to experience different ways of worshipping, by taking them to different events or churches. If the right relationships have been built up with young people they will be able to question, explore and reflect on the new experiences.

If we are going to help young people to 'stand before God and learn how to live', we need to allow them the second type of freedom, the freedom to explore and make mistakes, and to fail. Having worked with many young people I have realized that one of the key principles to learn is when to let them do something that you know is not quite going to turn out as they expect it to. The church environment should be a safe place in which to make these mistakes, even if it is going to have an effect on the Sunday service. This is all part of personal and faith development.

Respect

OK, so you might say this is a fourth principle, but respect should be key to all of the principles I have outlined. Young people are children becoming adults. We need to respect the views that they are forming, the ideas they have and the people they choose to build relationships with. We might not agree with some of them but we still need to respect them. It's not easy to say to the young people, 'I might not agree with what you are saying about a faith or life issue but I am going to respect you for standing up for it', but it helps the young people to start owning their faith.

As a young person growing up struggling with my faith and adolescence it was the relationships I formed and the freedom that my church and other church-related activities gave me helped me to explore and in the end own my faith.

'As a young person growing up struggling with my faith and adolescence it was the relationships I formed and the freedom that my church and other church-related activities gave me helped me to explore and in the end own my faith.'

THINKING IT THROUGH

1. How can you help the young people in your church to own their faith?
2. What room is there in your setting to offer activities other than a once-a-week group?
3. How often do you allow young people to have a say in the way that your services run?
4. How can you give the young people freedom in your church?
5. What significant relationships is your church building with the young people in your congregation?
6. How can you enable the building of relationships?
7. How has young people's culture changed from your adolescence?
8. What are the implications of young people having too much choice in today's society?
9. In what ways can you make your youth activities become a priority in young people's lives?
10. How can you foster participation by young people in your church?
11. How does your experience of church and youth groups affect your leadership style and faith journey?
12. Do you have a lifelong faith?

IS SUNDAY LINKED WITH MONDAY?

SUMMARY

Within this chapter I have outlined the principles that will help young people to have a faith that links Sunday to the rest of their lives. I recognize that for some churches these principles will be difficult to implement and might require a whole new mindset in the way that you work with young people. Please don't be put off doing something to help young people own their faith, but instead make small steps into doing something.

My hope is that you will foster a safe environment for young people to question, develop and ultimately own their faith and one in which they will choose to participate. I also hope that through the work that you do, young people see the link between Sunday and Monday and that they grow into lifelong worshipping disciples who choose to 'stand before God and learn how to live'.

IS SUNDAY LINKED WITH MONDAY?

TAKING IT FURTHER

George Barna, *Real Teens*, Regal, 2001.

Gavin Calver, *Disappointed with Jesus?*, Monarch, 2004.

Maxine Green, *Accompanying Young People on Their Spiritual Quest*, Church House Publishing, 1998.

Carol E. Lytch, *Choosing Church: What makes a difference for teens*, Westminster/John Knox Press, 2004.

www.barna.org – American research group looking at teenager issues.

NOTES

1 What is worship?

1. S. Conway and D. Stancliffe, *Living the Eucharist*, Darton, Longman & Todd, 2001, p. 3.

2 The place of music in worship

1. Matt Redman, 'When the music fades', *Intimacy – Track 8: The heart of worship*. Survivor Records, 1998.

3 Word of life? Prayer and word in work with young people

1. Mike Riddell, Mark Pierson and Cathy Kirkpatrick, in Tim E. Dearborn and Scott Coll (eds), *Worship at the Next Level: Insight from contemporary voices*, Baker Books, 2004, pp. 136–7.
2. Wild Goose Worship Group, *A Wee Worship Book, Fourth Incarnation*, Wild Goose Publications, 1999, p. 104.
3. M. Riddell in Pete Ward (ed.), *The Rite Stuff*, Bible Reading Fellowship, 2004, p. 89, emphasis mine.
4. T. Beaudoin, *Virtual Faith*, Jossey-Bass, 1998, p. 74.
5. Beaudoin, *Virtual Faith*, p. 32, quoting Cooke 1983, p. 32.
6. Ward, *The Rite Stuff*, p. 11.
7. Peter L. Berger, *A Rumour of Angels*, Penguin, 1969, p. 70.
8. 'Mad world', Michael Andrews ft. Gary Jules, *Trading Snakeoil for Wolf Tickets*, Sanctuary, 2004.
9. Riddell in Ward, *The Rite Stuff*, p. 82.

4 Rites and rituals in worship

1. Not for this chapter but for a more general discussion on the experiences of young people in worship.
2. At the 1998 Lambeth Conference, the Church was urged 'everywhere to work at expressing the unchanging Gospel of Christ in words, actions, names, customs, liturgies, which communicate relevantly to each contemporary society' (see www.lambethconference.org/resolutions/1998). At another presentation at the same Conference, the Anglican Church recognized the importance of young people in the Church. It put the ball firmly in the court of the Church itself (and the bishops particularly) to help young people 'find or maintain their spiritual home'.

3. *The One Sheeter*, Vol. 7, Issue 3. Reach, Reach Development Services, 2004.
4. Recent research has shown that on average preferred learning styles are 37% aural, 24% visual and 39% by doing (this final figure rises to 60% with men!)
5. How funny that we called it alternative worship and interesting that the term 'alternative worship' now gives rise to certain expectations regarding its rituals and format. In other words, something new and creative very quickly accrues ritual value.
6. These were more worship events than services.
7. The 'smorgasbord' approach, as coined by Bishop Michael Marshall some years ago! How similar this is to young people's eating habits of grazing, rather than sitting down to a meal.

5 Creative approaches to existing liturgy

1. Mark Earey, *Liturgical Worship*, Church House Publishing, 2002.

6 Young people and all-age worship

1. *Good News for Young People: The Church of England's National Youth Strategy*, General Synod of the Church of England, Church House Publishing, 2002, p. 6.
2. General Synod, *Youth A Part*, Church House Publishing, 1996, p. 63.
3. *Good News for Young People*, p. 6.
4. Jim Trood, 'Is all-age worship possible in the Church of England in the 21st century?', MA thesis, St John's College, Nottingham, 2002, pp. 29–31.

7 Experimenting with new forms of worship

1. Jackie Cray, *Seen and Heard*, Monarch, 1995, p. 44.
2. Cray, *Seen and Heard*, p. 40.

8 What's the link between 'youth church' and 'adult church'?

1. Pete Ward, *Youth Work and the Mission of God*, SPCK, 1997.
2. *Mission-shaped Church*, GS1523, Church House Publishing, 2004, p. 85.
3. Bishop Graham Cray, 3rd Academic Conference on Youth Ministry, Mansfield College, Oxford, January, 1999. As quoted in *Mission-shaped Church*, p. 80.
4. *Mission-shaped Church*, p. 108.
5. *Eternity – The Beginning*, Encounters on the Edge No. 4, Sheffield Centre, 2000.

6. Encounters on the Edge No. 4.
7. Kester Brewin, *The Complex Christ: Signs of emergence in the urban church*, SPCK, 2004, p. 78.
8. *A Measure for Measures: In mission and ministry: Report of the review of the dioceses, pastoral and related measures*, GS1528, Church House Publishing, 2004, para. 3.16.
9. *A Measure for Measures*, para. 3.24.
10. Graham Cray, *Youth Congregations and the Emerging Church*, Grove Booklet Ev57, Grove Books, 1998.

9 Alternative forms of worship

1. Jonny Baker and Doug Gay, with Jenny Brown, *Alternative Worship*, SPCK, 2003, p. vii.
2. www.freshworship.org/facts.html
3. Paul Roberts, *Alternative Worship in Church of England*, Grove Books, 1999, p. 19.
4. Graham Cray, *Postmodern Culture and Youth Discipleship: Commitment or looking cool*, Grove Books, 1998, p. 13.
5. *Mission-shaped Church*, GS1523, Church House Publishing, 2004.
6. Paul Fiddes, *Participating in God*, Darton, Longman & Todd, 2000, p. 270.
7. Chap Clark offers an excellent theology of youth ministry in Kenda Creasey Dean, Chapman Clark and Dave Rahn (eds), *Starting Right: Thinking theologically about youth ministry*, Zondervan, 2001, p. 42.
8. Mike Pilavachi, www.passionforyourname.com, 2004.
9. Hughes, www.passionforyourname.com, 2005.
10. Baker, Gay and Brown, *Alternative Worship*, p. 4.
11. Sally Dakin and Ian Tarrant, *Labyrinths and Prayer Stations*, Grove Books, 2004, p. 3.
12. Pete Greig and Dave Roberts, *Red Moon Rising*, Kingsway, 2004, p. 86.
13. Greig and Roberts, *Red Moon Rising*, p. 305.

10 What do we mean by 'spirituality'?

1. National Youth Agency, Consultation Paper, February 2005, www.nya.org.uk
2. A. Brown and J. Furlong, *Spiritual Development in Schools*, second edn, National Society, 1997, p. 4.
3. Chandu Christian, 'Spirituality', *Youth and Policy* 65, 1999.

4. R. Rolheiser, *Seeking Spirituality*, Hodder & Stoughton, 1998, p. 5.
5. A. H. Maslow, *Motivation and Personality*, Harper and Row, 1987, p. 22.
6. J. Macquarrie, *Paths in Spirituality*, SCM Press, 1972, p. 40.
7. J. P. Leighton, *The Principles and Practice of Community Youthwork*, second edn, Chester House, 1975, p. 75.
8. Leighton, *The Principles and Practice of Community Youthwork*, p. 77.
9. K. Young, *The Art of Youthwork*, Russell House, 1999, p. 252.
10. R. White and J. Wyn, *Rethinking Youth*, Sage, 1997, p. 65.
11. D. Hay and R. Nye, *The Spirit of the Child*, HarperCollins, 1998, p. 59.
12. National Youth Agency, *National Occupational Standards for Youthwork*, 2000, p. 25.
13. Larry Parsons, 'Youth work and the spark of the divine' at www.infed.org/christianyouthwork/spark_of_the_divine.htm
14. Hay and Nye, *The Spirit of the Child*.

Postscript: Is Sunday linked with Monday?

1. National Youth Agency, *National Occupational Standards for Youth Work*, 2000, p. iv.
2. Maxine Green, *Accompanying Young People on Their Spiritual Quest*, Church House Publishing, 1998.
3. Gavin Calver, *Disappointed with Jesus?*, Monarch, 2004.
4. Calver, *Disappointed with Jesus?*, p. 144.
5. Calver, *Disappointed with Jesus?*, p. 144.